FIRST PLACE™

MEMBER'S GUIDE

A CHRIST-CENTERED HEALTH PROGRAM

Gospel Light

FIRST PLACE

Gospel Light is a Christian publisher dedicated to serving the local church. We believe God's vision for Gospel Light is to provide church leaders with biblical, user-friendly materials that will help them evangelize, disciple and minister to children, youth and families.

It is our prayer that this Gospel Light resource will help you discover biblical truth for your own life and help you minister to others. May God richly bless you.

For a free catalog of resources from Gospel Light, please contact your Christian supplier or contact us at 1-800-4-GOSPEL or www.gospellight.com.

PUBLISHING STAFF

William T. Greig, Publisher
Dr. Elmer L. Towns, Senior Consulting Publisher
Pam Weston, Senior Editor
Patti Pennington Virtue, Associate Editor
Jeff Kempton, Editorial Assistant
Hilary Young, Editorial Assistant
Kyle Duncan, Associate Publisher
Bayard Taylor, M.Div., Senior Editor, Biblical and Theological Issues
Dr. Gary S. Greig, Senior Advisor, Biblical and Theological Issues
Barbara LeVan Fisher, Cover Designer
Samantha A. Hsu, Designer

ISBN 0-8307-2868-6
© 2001 First Place
All rights reserved.
Printed in the U.S.A.

CAUTION

The information contained in this book is intended to be solely informational and educational. It is assumed that the First Place participant will consult a medical or health professional before beginning this or any other weight-loss or physical fitness program.

COPYRIGHT NOTICE

Do not make any copies of this book unless you adhere strictly to the guidelines found on this page. **Only pages with the following notation can be legally reproduced:**

ABOUT THE AUTHORS

Carole Lewis is the national director of First Place—a Christ-centered health program based at Houston's First Baptist Church. A leader at conferences and retreats throughout the country, Carole was a member of the original First Place group in 1981 at First Baptist, Houston. She became the full-time director in 1987.

Kay Smith, the associate national director of First Place, has been on the staff of Houston's First Baptist Church since 1987 and has served on a church staff since 1976. A speaker at retreats, seminars and conferences, Kay has lost 90 pounds on the First Place program.

Nancy Taylor has been the national leadership training director for First Place since 1997. She teaches leadership principles to First Place leaders throughout the country. She is a gracious speaker who delights her audiences with humor and encourages them with boldness.

Diane Coe is an energetic freelance communications specialist with 15 years experience in various aspects of communication and advertising services. Her most recent experience has been as a technical/medical writer. Diane wrote the maintenance section of this Member's Guide.

William J. (Jody) Wilkinson, M.D., M.S., wrote the Wellness Worksheets for this book. A physician and exercise physiologist at The Cooper Institute in Dallas, Texas, Dr. Wilkinson also serves as the Director of the Cooper Institute Weight Management Research Center. He strongly believes in using biblical teaching to motivate people to take care of their physical bodies and enjoy abundant living.

CONTENTS

Welcome to First Place 7
A Christ-Centered Health Program 8
The Nine Commitments 9

Prayer
    Establishing a Quiet Time 13
    Prayer Journaling: A Personal Testimony 15
    Weekly Prayer Request Sample Page 16
    Prayer Journal Sample 17

Scripture Reading and Bible Study
    Making the Most of Bible Study 18
    Scripture Reading Plan 19
    Hiding God's Word in Your Heart 23
    Sharing Your Faith 26
    Steps to Becoming a Christian 29

Live-It Food Plan
    Recommendations for Nutritional Health 31
    The Food Guide Pyramid 33
    Finding Your Healthy Weight 34
    Choosing a Calorie Level 37
    Calorie Level Exchanges 38
    Using the Commitment Record 40
    Using the Food Exchanges 43
    Live-It Plan 44
    Live-It: The Vegetarian Way 65
    Eating on the Go 67

Fitness and Activity
    Physical Activity Program 74
    The Activity Pyramid 79
    How Physically Active Are You? 82
    Testing Your Health-Related Fitness 85
    Starting a Walking Program 91
    Running Your Way to Health and Fitness 93
    Bicycling Your Way to Health and Fitness 96
    Water Exercise for Fitness and Health 99
    Monitoring Your Exercise Intensity 102
    Fitting in Strength Training 105
    A Flexible Fitness Program 108

Health Assessment

    Understanding Weight Gain and Obesity—Part I 111

    Understanding Weight Gain and Obesity—Part II 115

    Understanding Weight Gain and Obesity—Part III 118

    Understanding Your Eating Habits 121

Nutrition

    What's the Big Deal About Water? 129

    Understanding the Nutrition Facts Panel 132

    Sugar: Sweetness by Any Other Name 135

    The Anytime, Anywhere Restaurant Guide 138

    Changing Recipes 141

    Meatless Meals 144

    Calculating Exchanges for a Recipe 147

    Recipe Conversion Chart 148

    Preventing Osteoporosis 149

    The Truth About Fats 152

    Choosing High-Fiber Foods 155

    Off to a Good Start 158

Maintenance

    Maintaining Your Healthy Weight 161

    At-Goal Form 163

    Running to Win 165

    Reviewing His Provision 167

    The Balancing Act 169

    Standing on Firm Ground 172

    Taking Aim 174

    My New Daily Exchange Allowances 176

    Keeping Track to Keep *on* Track 177

    Encouraging One Another 179

    Becoming an Overcomer 182

    Keeping First Things First 184

WELCOME TO FIRST PLACE

The First Place program is the result of a godly desire placed in the hearts of a group of Christians to establish a Christ-centered weight control program. The basic question that initiated their search was *Since God has saved us from our sins and given us an abundant life, why can't we, as Christians, use that same power in the area of weight control?*

With that question in mind, they began to develop a program that would meet the needs of Christians who needed to get their weight under control. Little did they know what they were undertaking! It was an immense assignment, but knowing God had called them to the task, they placed all of their hopes and aspirations in Him and began the project. They prayed, studied, prayed, read, prayed, wrote—and First Place began to take shape!

They knew that the program needed to include Bible study, small-group support, accountability, a proven commonsense nutrition plan, exercise, record keeping and many other elements to be effective. They knew putting Christ first in their lives would be the success of the program. Their aim was for growth in all areas of a person's life: spiritual, mental, emotional and physical.

Matthew 6:33: "Seek first his kingdom and his righteousness, and all these things will be given to you as well" was chosen as the theme verse for the program. Hence, the name First Place.

The original First Place groups met in the spring of 1981 at First Baptist Church of Houston, Texas. What began as a Christ-centered weight loss program has evolved into a nationally recognized total health program. Today the First Place program is used in every state and many foreign countries. Thousands of lives have been changed radically through the power of Christ.

We praise God for the leadership He provided as all of the steps of First Place were planned and penned. Our greatest desire was, and continues to be, that God will receive all the glory, honor and praise and that as a result of First Place, individuals will live healthier, happier and more abundant lives with God as their first priority.

May God always have first place in your life.

A Christ-Centered Health Program

Balance

Jesus said, "I have come that they may have life, and have it to the full" (John 10:10). Life becomes abundant when Christ has first place. Abundant living means being in good condition spiritually, mentally, emotionally and physically. That's what First Place is all about. It is a total Christ-centered health program, emphasizing balance in all four areas of life.

Luke 2:52 states that "Jesus grew in wisdom and stature, and in favor with God and men." Our Lord developed mentally (wisdom), physically (stature), spiritually (favor with God) and emotionally (favor with men). If our Lord developed in these four areas, then we should seek to do the same.

Bread

In John 6:35, Jesus described Himself as "the bread of life. He who comes to me will never go hungry." It is through our daily dependence on Jesus that we can achieve balance in all four areas of life. The First Place program is meant to be a daily process. Some days will be better than others, but no matter what, we need to keep Christ in each day and remember that He is the One who satisfies our hunger. How does He do that?

Bible

In Matthew 4:4, Jesus explained that God's Word is central to true satisfaction: "It is written: 'Man does not live on bread alone, but on every word that comes from the mouth of God.' "

One of the main ways God communicates with us is through His Word, the Bible. Studying God's Word contains guidelines for developing physical well-being, equipping us mentally to make right choices, providing emotional stability to handle everyday circumstances as well as crisis situations, and growing spiritually as we deepen our relationships with Him.

THE NINE COMMITMENTS

The First Place program has nine commitments that will help you draw closer to the Lord and aid you in establishing a solid and consistent Christian life. Each commitment is a necessary and important part of the goal of First Place to help you become healthier and stronger in all areas of your life—becoming the person God created you to be.

To help you achieve growth in all four areas, First Place asks you to keep these nine commitments:

1. Attendance
2. Encouragement
3. Prayer
4. Bible Reading
5. Scripture Memory Verse
6. Bible Study
7. Live-It
8. Commitment Record (CR)
9. Exercise

COMMITMENT ONE: ATTENDANCE

Attend Your Weekly Meeting

Jesus commanded us in John 13:34 "Love one another. As I have loved you, so you must love one another." In First Place, you can model love for others by attending the weekly group meeting. Attendance will provide accountability as you seek to reach your First Place goals. Faithful attendance for the next 13 weeks must be your priority. Arriving on time and staying for the entire one hour and 15 minute meeting is important. Occasions may arise when you must miss a class; that's understandable. However, please call your leader or a fellow class member if you will be absent.

COMMITMENT TWO: ENCOURAGEMENT

Encourage One Person in Your Group Weekly

Ecclesiastes 4:12 states: "Though one may be overpowered, two can defend themselves." You are asked to encourage a fellow group member through a phone call, e-mail, fax, postcard, etc. You may also reach out to another group member when you need encouragement. At times, the name of someone in your group may come to mind—don't neglect to contact that person. Often this is the Holy Spirit prompting you to reach out to someone who needs your encouragement.

COMMITMENT THREE: PRAYER

Set a Daily Time for Prayer

God instructs us in Psalm 46:10 to "be still, and know that I am God." You will find a feast of spiritual blessings as you learn to communicate with Him.

- **Group meeting prayer time**—Ephesians 6:18 says: "Pray in the Spirit on all occasions with all kinds of prayers and requests. With this in mind, be alert and always keep on praying for all the saints." You will spend time in prayer at your weekly meeting. Your prayer requests should be short and specific, relating to your personal needs. All group prayer requests must be kept confidential.

- **Personal prayer time**—Colossians 4:2 says: "Devote yourselves to prayer, being watchful and thankful." Included in your Bible study book are prayer request pages to record group members' prayer requests. Pray daily for fellow members and your leader. Pray also for your own commitments and for God's help in every area of your life. Refer to Establishing a Quiet Time on page 13.

- **Pray continually**—1 Thessalonians 5:17,18 says: "Pray continually; give thanks in all circumstances, for this is God's will for you in Christ Jesus." You can pray at any and all times during the day. Pray when you are tempted in any area of your life. Arm yourself with prayer and watch how God works.

COMMITMENT FOUR: BIBLE READING

Write God's Word on Your Heart

In Psalm 32:8, God promises, "I will instruct you and teach you in the way you should go; I will counsel you and watch over you." First Place has provided a suggested Scripture reading plan that includes a daily selection from both the Old Testament and the New Testament (pp. 19-22). This plan, as any other, is most valuable when used regularly. The text included for each day can be read thoughtfully in 15 to 30 minutes. Reading through the *One Year Bible* (Tyndale House) or participating in an in-depth Bible study could also fulfill the Bible-reading commitment.

In John 8:32, Jesus said, "You will know the truth, and the truth will set you free." The purpose of the Scripture reading commitment is not to study the Bible but to keep you in God's Word daily. Don't be concerned about the length of your daily Bible readings. Ask God to speak to your heart and allow the Holy Spirit to reveal truths as you make yourself available. As you read God's Word regularly, you will lay a foundation for spiritual development.

COMMITMENT FIVE: SCRIPTURE MEMORY VERSE

Memorize One Verse Each Week

God's Word lifts and strengthens us as we walk with Him daily. Psalm 119:105, states that the Word of God is "a lamp to my feet and a light for my path." God's written Word will be a light to guide your life, but you must know His Word for it to be a light for your path.

As part of the First Place program, you are asked to memorize one verse every week and review it daily. You will quote this verse when you weigh in each week. The memory verse corresponds with the Bible study. Commit it to memory so you can say along with the psalmist, "I have hidden your word in my heart that I might not sin against you" (Psalm 119:11).

There are Scripture memory aids provided in the Bible study book to help you, including Scripture memory verses in each week's Bible study and the Scripture memory CD inside the back cover.

COMMITMENT SIX: BIBLE STUDY

Study God's Word

In 2 Timothy 2:15, Paul instructed, "Do your best to present yourself to God as one approved, a workman who does not need to be ashamed and who correctly handles the word of truth." The first two weeks of each session will introduce you to the Live-It food exchange plan. You will begin the Bible study after your second meeting. The First Place Bible study is not meant to be an intense study. The questions are short and related to your total health. Each day you should read, meditate and answer only one day's portion of that week's Bible study. Each week includes five days of Bible study with two days of reflection and review. You will want to come to each group meeting prepared to discuss what truths God has revealed to you that week in Bible study.

Consistency is the key in Bible study. You would never save up all of the food that you were allotted to eat for one week and eat it all the night before you weigh in at your First Place meeting. In the same way, you would not benefit from completing the entire week of Bible study in one day. In other words, don't cram down your spiritual food all in one sitting.

COMMITMENT SEVEN: LIVE-IT

Follow the Live-It Healthy Food Plan

The term "Live-It" was chosen for the food plan because the First Place plan is meant to be lived for a lifetime. On the other hand, diets are usually a temporary solution to a lifelong problem. Live-It is a healthy eating plan recommended by credible health professionals. It is designed to help members reach and maintain their healthy weight, meet nutritional requirements, promote good health, lead active lives and reduce chronic disease risks.

Live-It will be explained in a video shown at your first two meetings. The food lists are based on the USDA Food Guide Pyramid. First Place recommends eating three balanced meals each day with optional healthy snacks. In this plan, a well-balanced meal includes certain amounts of foods from each of the following food groups: meats, vegetables, fruits, breads, milk and fats.

Avoid Sugar and Foods with Added Sugar

First Place cautions against eating sugar in large amounts and against frequent snacks of foods and beverages containing sugar. Sugary foods supply unnecessary calories and few nutrients. Ironically, many fat-free products are loaded with extra sugar.

Many First Place members have found that sugar triggers eating binges that are very difficult to control; therefore, they have decided to eliminate sugar from their diets. On the other hand, some First Place members find consuming sugar in moderation keeps them from feeling deprived. The goal is to consume all the recommended nutrients each day without consuming too many calories.

Using Sugar Substitutes

Because of the unknown effects of artificial sweeteners, First Place recommends that members use sugar substitutes in moderation.

COMMITMENT EIGHT: COMMITMENT RECORD (CR)

Keep a Record of Your Nine Commitments

The Commitment Record is a personal record of the nine commitments you keep each week. It is a self-evaluation record that reflects strengths and areas that need improvement. The CR is an accountability tool, not a binding chain. Keeping a record is an opportunity to reflect on how well you are caring for God's temple.

Your CR will be handed in at each weekly meeting. The leader will evaluate your progress to help, encourage and motivate you. Don't push yourself toward perfection; that's not the ultimate goal. Remember this journey toward wholeness will be achieved one step at a time.

For further reference, you will find sample CRs in the materials (pp. 40-42). At the first meeting, you will learn how to fill out this form.

COMMITMENT NINE: EXERCISE

Exercise Three to Five Times Weekly

In 1 Corinthians 3:16, Paul reminded us, "Don't you know that you yourselves are God's temple and that God's Spirit lives in you?" Exercise is maintenance for your body, God's home. For those who need to get fit, the commitment in First Place is to exercise five times each week. For those desiring to maintain fitness, the commitment is a minimum of three times each week. Further, it is recommended that you don't go more than 48 hours without exercising.

The three necessary components of healthy exercise are: aerobic activity, strength training and flexibility. The First Place materials will help you evaluate your fitness level and develop a personal exercise plan. The Scripture Memory CD is designed to be used during exercise. Each CD is designed to be used during a workout; the first song was composed with a warm-up tempo. The next eight songs were written with increasing intensity for a steady aerobic beat and the tenth song has a tempo that encourages a cool-down period.

Prayer

ESTABLISHING A QUIET TIME

TIME ALONE WITH GOD

Time

> *Very early in the morning, while it was still dark, Jesus got up, left the house and went off to a*
> *solitary place, where he prayed* (Mark 1:35).

First Place recommends that you rise 30 minutes to an hour earlier than usual to spend time with God and receive strength and guidance for the day ahead. If this is absolutely impossible, then find a time during the day to spend time alone with God. Consistency is the key to establishing a rich devotional life full of power and answers to life's problems.

Place

> *When you pray, go into your room, close the door and pray to your Father, who is unseen.*
> *Then your Father, who sees what is done in secret, will reward you* (Matthew 6:6).

Choose a place where you can be alone with God each day. Keep your Bible, journal and pen in this same location.

HOW TO HAVE AN EFFECTIVE QUIET TIME

After you have chosen the time and place to meet God daily, follow these steps for a fruitful and worshipful time with the Lord.

Clear Your Heart and Mind

Begin your quiet time by reading the daily selection from a devotional guide such as *My Utmost for His Highest* by Oswald Chambers—a favorite of many First Place members. Of course, you can use any devotional that has a strong emphasis of Scripture and prayer.

> *Be still and know that [He is] God* (Psalm 46:10).

Scripture Reading

Pray, asking God to reveal through the reading of His Word something that you need for the day. Spend time reading and meditating on an idea or a passage. Always try to find a nugget to encourage or direct you through the day.

I have hidden your word in my heart that I might not sin against you (Psalm 119:11).

To read Scripture in a more systematic and structured manner, ask yourself the following questions, looking carefully for the answers as you read that day's selection.

1. Is there

- → Sin to confess?
- → A promise to claim?
- → An example to follow?
- → A command to obey?
- → A situation to avoid?

2. How should I respond to what I've read today?

Write Your Prayers Using the Acronym A.C.T.S.

Adore and Affirm God as Lord

Praise God for who He is. For example, "I praise You, Lord, for being the Creator of the universe." You can adore and affirm God through song, poetry or specific Scripture. The psalms are full of adoration and praise.

O LORD, our LORD, how majestic is your name in all the earth! (Psalm 8:1)

Confession of Sin

Confession means agreeing with God that what you have done or neglected to do is against His perfect will. After you confess your known sin, ask God to reveal hidden sins.

If we confess our sins, he is faithful and just and will

forgive us our sins and purify us from all unrighteousness (1 John 1:9).

Thanksgiving

Thank God daily for how He is working in your life. Thank Him for the blessings and the trials.

Give thanks in all circumstances, for this is God's will for you in Christ Jesus (1 Thessalonians 5:18).

Supplication

Ask God to meet your needs or the needs of someone else. Always ask according to God's will.

The prayer of a righteous man is powerful and effective (James 5:16).

PRAYER JOURNALING

A PERSONAL TESTIMONY

Believing that God wants His children to pray, I began writing my prayers in April 1990. For several years, I had resisted praying in this manner. Being a fun-loving individual, I felt that writing my prayers would be time consuming to say the least. At that time, my prayer life was not something I found pleasant or rewarding; I felt five minutes was a long time to pray. My thoughts would begin to wander and before I knew it, I was planning the day ahead. I had attended seminars on prayer for years. I thought some secret formula must exist that would make me a mighty prayer warrior.

The greatest benefit I have received from writing my prayers is the total focus on praying while I am writing. My mind is focused because it is difficult to write and think of other things at the same time. Also, the Holy Spirit directs my praying when my mind is tuned in to God. My faith grows tremendously as I go back through my journal and highlight the many answers to prayer in my life.

God has taught me many truths through journaling. I have learned to praise Him in all things. Trials in my life may seem like roadblocks to me, but God sees these trials as stepping stones to victory and spiritual growth. Journaling has taught me that God hears and answers all my prayers. When I pray within the framework of God's will, His answer is always a resounding yes! When God tells me no, He does so because I have asked something contrary to His will for my life. Many times His no is only "Wait, my child—the timing is not yet right."

Another lesson I learned when writing my prayers is how the Holy Spirit brings to mind sin that hinders my fellowship with God. Sin in me affects everyone I meet. I have learned that by confessing and turning from my sin, I am immediately restored and able to be used in God's service.

Thanksgiving is a very important part of my prayers. While praise is expressing gratitude for who God *is*, thanksgiving is gratitude to God for what He *does*. If we, as earthly parents, love to hear the words "thank you" from our children, how much more God wants us to thank Him for His blessings. Most of God's greatest blessings do not cost a penny. Money can't buy a glorious sunset or a walk on the beach. Good health is a blessing many people would pay much to attain. God blesses us in hundreds of ways each day. I praise God for who He *is* and thank Him for what He *does* in my life.

God also has taught me the importance of intercession in my life as a Christian. The Holy Spirit often breaks loose in others' lives as a discernable result of the prayers of believing Christians. What a joy to see healing and restoration take place in the lives of those we love and know.

Because of what God can do in your life, I recommend that you begin writing your prayers during your participation in First Place. Members will need to purchase a prayer journal. My prayer is that God will use this process to help you focus your attention on Him as you pray. God bless you as you begin writing your prayers.

Carole Lewis
First Place National Director

Sample of Weekly Prayer Request Page

In Matthew 18:19, Jesus says, *"Again, I tell you that if two of you on earth agree about anything you ask for, it will be done for you by my Father in heaven."*

Use the Group Prayer Requests page located at the end of each week in the Bible study to record your First Place members' prayer requests. Record:

- Name of person requesting prayer
- Request
- Date the prayer is answered

The goal of the class prayer time is to pray for requests that are affecting your daily life. As the group bonds, the class becomes a safe place to share confidential requests.

GROUP PRAYER REQUESTS   TODAY'S DATE: _2/16/01_

NAME	REQUEST	RESULTS
Joyce	Biopsy on Thursday	1/18-benign
Bill	Sale of house	2/15-sold!
Stacy	Sugar free this week	1/18-did it!

Prayer Journal Sample

Use your prayer journal to record your personal prayers and thoughts. You might like to include some of the following:

- ➤ Record your prayers to God.
- ➤ Express your praise and thankfulness to God.
- ➤ Confess sins.
- ➤ Write out your personal requests.
- ➤ Write as much or as little as you like—quality, not quantity, is what matters.

1/25/01

Dear Lord,

I praise you today, for you are my Creator! You are holy, righteous and just. I love you and want to seek you first today in all that I do. You are my all!

Lord, you have searched my heart and you know all of my ways. Father, forgive me for being so selfish and not reaching out to those around me. I have been caught up in my own problems and haven't been concerned about those around me. Lord, today I commit to you to reach out in love to Martha, my fellow First Place member.

Thank you, Lord, for giving me such caring and loving friends and family. They are a gift from you. Lord, I ask that you would help me keep my commitment of reaching out to Martha and provide a way for me to minister to her.

Lord, also, put a guard over my mouth today and enable me to see the way of escape from the temptations I will face as I eat out today with my coworkers. I love you.

Your daughter,

Nancy

Scripture Reading and Bible Study

MAKING THE MOST OF BIBLE STUDY

- Set aside 15 to 20 minutes each day to complete the daily Bible study assignment. It's best not to attempt to complete a week's worth of Bible study in one day.
- Pray before each day's study and ask God to give you understanding and a teachable heart.
- Keep in mind that the ultimate goal of Bible study is not for knowledge only but also for application and a changed life.
- First Place suggests using the *New International Version* to complete the studies.
- Don't feel anxious if you can't seem to find the correct answer. Many times the Word will speak differently to different people, depending upon where they are in their walk with God and the season of life they are experiencing.
- Be prepared to discuss with your fellow First Place members what you learned that week through the Bible study.

SCRIPTURE READING PLAN

The following plan will guide you through an Old Testament and New Testament passage each day. You will read through the Bible in one year if you follow this plan. Each reading will take approximately 15-30 minutes to complete.

To use these pages, remove them from this guide and fold them into a booklet that can be inserted into your Bible.

JANUARY

1   Genesis 1—3; Matthew 1
2   Genesis 4—6; Matthew 2:1-12
3   Genesis 7—8; Matthew 2:13-23
4   Genesis 9—11; Matthew 3
5   Genesis 12—14; Matthew 4:1-11
6   Genesis 15—17; Matthew 4:12-25
7   Genesis 18—19; Matthew 5:1-16
8   Genesis 20—22; Matthew 5:17-48
9   Genesis 23—24; Matthew 6:1-18
10 Genesis 25—27; Matthew 6:19-34
11 Genesis 28—29; Matthew 7:1-14
12 Genesis 30—31; Matthew 7:15-29
13 Genesis 32—33; Matthew 8:1-17
14 Genesis 34—36; Matthew 8:18-34
15 Genesis 37—38; Matthew 9:1-26
16 Genesis 39—40; Matthew 9:27-38
17 Genesis 41—42; Matthew 10
18 Genesis 43—45; Matthew 11:1-19
19 Genesis 46—47; Matthew 11:20-30
20 Genesis 48—50; Matthew 12:1-21
21 Exodus 1—2; Matthew 12:22-50
22 Exodus 3—4; Matthew 13:1-23
23 Exodus 5—7; Matthew 13:24-58
24 Exodus 8—9; Matthew 14:1-21
25 Exodus 10—11; Matthew 14:22-36
26 Exodus 12—13; Matthew 15:1-20
27 Exodus 14—15; Matthew 15:21-39
28 Exodus 16—18; Matthew 16:1-12
29 Exodus 19—21; Matthew 16:13-28
30 Exodus 22—23; Matthew 17:1-13
31 Exodus 24—26; Matthew 17:14-27

FEBRUARY

1 Exodus 27—28; Matthew 18:1-20
2 Exodus 29—30; Matthew 18:21-35
3 Exodus 31—32; Matthew 19:1-15
4 Exodus 33—34; Matthew 19:16-30
5 Exodus 35—36; Matthew 20:1-16
6 Exodus 37—38; Matthew 20:17-34
7 Exodus 39—40; Matthew 21:1-22
8 Leviticus 1—3; Matthew 21:23-46
9 Leviticus 4—5; Matthew 22:1-14
10 Leviticus 6—8; Matthew 22:15-46
11 Leviticus 9—10; Matthew 23
12 Leviticus 11—13; Matthew 24:1-31
13 Leviticus 14—15; Matthew 24:32-51
14 Leviticus 16—18; Matthew 25:1-30
15 Leviticus 19—20; Matthew 25:31-46
16 Leviticus 21—23; Matthew 26:1-35
17 Leviticus 24—25; Matthew 26:36-56
18 Leviticus 26—27; Matthew 26:57-75
19 Numbers 1—2; Matthew 27:1-31
20 Numbers 3—4; Matthew 27:32-66
21 Numbers 5—6; Matthew 28
22 Numbers 7; Mark 1:1-15
23 Numbers 8—10; Mark 1:16-45
24 Numbers 11—12; Mark 2:1-12
25 Numbers 13—14; Mark 2:13-28
26 Numbers 15—16; Mark 3:1-12
27 Numbers 17—18; Mark 3:13-35
28 Numbers 19—20; Mark 4:1-20
29 Numbers 21; Mark 4:21-41

MARCH

1 Numbers 22—24; Mark 5:1-20
2 Numbers 25—26; Mark 5:21-43
3 Numbers 27—29; Mark 6:1-13
4 Numbers 30—31; Mark 6:14-32
5 Numbers 32—33; Mark 6:33-56
6 Numbers 34—36; Mark 7:1-23
7 Deuteronomy 1—2; Mark 7:24-37
8 Deuteronomy 3—4; Mark 8:1-10
9 Deuteronomy 5—6; Mark 8:11-26
10 Deuteronomy 7—9; Mark 8:27-38
11 Deuteronomy 10—11; Mark 9:1-13
12 Deuteronomy 12—14; Mark 9:14-29
13 Deuteronomy 15—17; Mark 9:30-50
14 Deuteronomy 18—20; Mark 10:1-16
15 Deuteronomy 21—23; Mark 10:17-31
16 Deuteronomy 24—26; Mark 10:32-52
17 Deuteronomy 27—28; Mark 11:1-11
18 Deuteronomy 29—30; Mark 11:12-33
19 Deuteronomy 31—32; Mark 12:1-12
20 Deuteronomy 33—34; Mark 12:13-27
21 Joshua 1—2; Mark 12:28-44
22 Joshua 3—4; Mark 13:1-13
23 Joshua 5—6; Mark 13:14-37
24 Joshua 7—8; Mark 14:1-11
25 Joshua 9—10; Mark 14:12-31
26 Joshua 11—12; Mark 14:32-52
27 Joshua 13—15; Mark 14:53-72
28 Joshua 16—18; Mark 15:1-15
29 Joshua 19—20; Mark 15:16-39
30 Joshua 21—22; Mark 15:40-47
31 Joshua 23—24; Mark 16

DECEMBER

1 Daniel 5—6; 2 Peter 3
2 Daniel 7—8; 1 John 1
3 Daniel 9; 1 John 2
4 Daniel 10—12; 1 John 3
5 Hosea 1—3; 1 John 4
6 Hosea 4—6; 1 John 5
7 Hosea 7—8; 2 John
8 Hosea 9—10; 3 John
9 Hosea 11—12; Jude
10 Hosea 13—14; Revelation 1
11 Joel; Revelation 2
12 Amos 1—2; Revelation 3
13 Amos 3—4; Revelation 4
14 Amos 5—7; Revelation 5
15 Amos 8—9; Revelation 6
16 Obadiah; Revelation 7
17 Jonah; Revelation 8
18 Micah 1—2; Revelation 9
19 Micah 3—4; Revelation 10
20 Micah 5—7; Revelation 11
21 Nahum; Revelation 12
22 Habakkuk; Revelation 13
23 Zephaniah; Revelation 14
24 Haggai; Revelation 15
25 Zechariah 1—3; Revelation 16
26 Zechariah 4—5; Revelation 17
27 Zechariah 6—8; Revelation 18
28 Zechariah 9—11; Revelation 19
29 Zechariah 12—14; Revelation 20
30 Malachi 1—2; Revelation 21
31 Malachi 3—4; Revelation 22

OCTOBER

1 Jeremiah 1, Ephesians 1
2 Jeremiah 2; Ephesians 2
3 Jeremiah 3—4; Ephesians 3
4 Jeremiah 5—6; Ephesians 4
5 Jeremiah 7—8; Ephesians 5
6 Jeremiah 9—10; Ephesians 6
7 Jeremiah 11—12; Philippians 1
8 Jeremiah 13—14; Philippians 2
9 Jeremiah 15—17; Philippians 3
10 Jeremiah 18—19; Philippians 4
11 Jeremiah 20—21; Colossians 1
12 Jeremiah 22—23; Colossians 2
13 Jeremiah 24—25; Colossians 3
14 Jeremiah 26; Colossians 4
15 Jeremiah 27—28; 1 Thessalonians 1
16 Jeremiah 29—30; 1 Thessalonians 2
17 Jeremiah 31; 1 Thessalonians 3
18 Jeremiah 32; 1 Thessalonians 4
19 Jeremiah 33—34; 1 Thessalonians 5
20 Jeremiah 35—36; 2 Thessalonians 1
21 Jeremiah 37—38; 2 Thessalonians 2
22 Jeremiah 39—41; 2 Thessalonians 3
23 Jeremiah 42—43; 1 Timothy 1
24 Jeremiah 44—45; 1 Timothy 2
25 Jeremiah 46—47; 1 Timothy 3
26 Jeremiah 48; 1 Timothy 4
27 Jeremiah 49; 1 Timothy 5
28 Jeremiah 50; 1 Timothy 6
29 Jeremiah 51; 2 Timothy 1
30 Jeremiah 52; 2 Timothy 2
31 Lamentations 1; 2 Timothy 3

NOVEMBER

1 Lamentations 2; 2 Timothy 4
2 Lamentations 3; Titus 1
3 Lamentations 4; Titus 2
4 Lamentations 5; Titus 3
5 Ezekiel 1—2; Philemon
6 Ezekiel 3—5; Hebrews 1
7 Ezekiel 6—7; Hebrews 2
8 Ezekiel 8—10; Hebrews 3
9 Ezekiel 11—12; Hebrews 4
10 Ezekiel 13—14; Hebrews 5
11 Ezekiel 15—16; Hebrews 6
12 Ezekiel 17—18; Hebrews 7
13 Ezekiel 19—20; Hebrews 8
14 Ezekiel 21—22; Hebrews 9
15 Ezekiel 23—24; Hebrews 10
16 Ezekiel 25—26; Hebrews 11
17 Ezekiel 27—28; Hebrews 12
18 Ezekiel 29—30; Hebrews 13
19 Ezekiel 31—32; James 1
20 Ezekiel 33—34; James 2
21 Ezekiel 35—37; James 3
22 Ezekiel 38—39; James 4
23 Ezekiel 40—41; James 5
24 Ezekiel 42—43; 1 Peter 1
25 Ezekiel 44—46; 1 Peter 2
26 Ezekiel 47—48; 1 Peter 3
27 Daniel 1; 1 Peter 4
28 Daniel 2; 1 Peter 5
29 Daniel 3; 2 Peter 1
30 Daniel 4; 2 Peter 2

APRIL

1 Judges 1—3; Luke 1:1-25
2 Judges 4—5; Luke 1:26-38
3 Judges 6; Luke 1:39-56
4 Judges 7—8; Luke 1:57-80
5 Judges 9; Luke 2:1-20
6 Judges 10—12; Luke 2:21-40
7 Judges 13—15; Luke 2:41-52
8 Judges 16; Luke 3:1-20
9 Judges 17—18; Luke 3:21-38
10 Judges 19—20; Luke 4:1-13
11 Judges 21; Luke 4:14-32
12 Ruth 1—2; Luke 4:33-44
13 Ruth 3—4; Luke 5:1-26
14 1 Samuel 1—2; Luke 5:27-39
15 1 Samuel 3—4; Luke 6:1-11
16 1 Samuel 5—6; Luke 6:12-49
17 1 Samuel 7—8; Luke 7:1-17
18 1 Samuel 9—10; Luke 7:18-35
19 1 Samuel 11—13; Luke 7:36-50
20 1 Samuel 14—15; Luke 8:1-18
21 1 Samuel 16—17; Luke 8:19-39
22 1 Samuel 18—19; Luke 8:40-56
23 1 Samuel 20—21; Luke 9:1-17
24 1 Samuel 22—23; Luke 9:18-45
25 1 Samuel 24—25; Luke 9:46-62
26 1 Samuel 26—27; Luke 10:1-24
27 1 Samuel 28—29; Luke 10:25-42
28 1 Samuel 30—31; Luke 11:1-13
29 2 Samuel 1—2; Luke 11:14-28
30 2 Samuel 3—4; Luke 11:29-54

MAY

1 2 Samuel 5—6; Luke 12:1-12
2 2 Samuel 7—8; Luke 12:13-34
3 2 Samuel 9—10; Luke 12:35-59
4 2 Samuel 11—12; Luke 13:1-17
5 2 Samuel 13—14; Luke 13:18-35
6 2 Samuel 15—16; Luke 14:1-24
7 2 Samuel 17—18; Luke 14:25-35
8 2 Samuel 19—20; Luke 15
9 2 Samuel 21—22; Luke 16:1-18
10 2 Samuel 23—24; Luke 16:19-31
11 1 Kings 1—2; Luke 17:1-19
12 1 Kings 3—4; Luke 17:20-37
13 1 Kings 5—6; Luke 18:1-17
14 1 Kings 7—8; Luke 18:18-43
15 1 Kings 9—11; Luke 19:1-27
16 1 Kings 12—13; Luke 19:28-48
17 1 Kings 14—15; Luke 20:1-26
18 1 Kings 16—17; Luke 20:27-47
19 1 Kings 18—19; Luke 21:1-28
20 1 Kings 20—21; Luke 21:29-38
21 1 Kings 22; Luke 22:1-23
22 2 Kings 1—3; Luke 22:24-53
23 2 Kings 4—5; Luke 22:54-71
24 2 Kings 6—7; Luke 23:1-12
25 2 Kings 8—9; Luke 23:13-32
26 2 Kings 10—11; Luke 23:33-56
27 2 Kings 12—13; Luke 24:1-12
28 2 Kings 14—15; Luke 24:13-53
29 2 Kings 16—17; John 1:1-18
30 2 Kings 18—20; John 1:19-51
31 2 Kings 21—23; John 2

JUNE

1. 2 Kings 24—25; John 3:1-21
2. 1 Chronicles 1—2; John 3:22-36
3. 1 Chronicles 3—4; John 4:1-42
4. 1 Chronicles 5—6; John 4:43-54
5. 1 Chronicles 7—8; John 5:1-17
6. 1 Chronicles 9—10; John 5:18-47
7. 1 Chronicles 11—12; John 6:1-15
8. 1 Chronicles 13—15; John 6:16-40
9. 1 Chronicles 16—17; John 6:41-71
10. 1 Chronicles 18—19; John 7:1-36
11. 1 Chronicles 20—21; John 7:37-52
12. 1 Chronicles 22—24; John 8:1-11
13. 1 Chronicles 25—27; John 8:12-59
14. 1 Chronicles 28—29; John 9
15. 2 Chronicles 1—2; John 10:1-21
16. 2 Chronicles 3—4; John 10:22-42
17. 2 Chronicles 5—6; John 11
18. 2 Chronicles 7—9; John 12:1-19
19. 2 Chronicles 10—12; John 12:20-50
20. 2 Chronicles 13—16; John 13
21. 2 Chronicles 17—19; John 14
22. 2 Chronicles 20—21; John 15
23. 2 Chronicles 22—23; John 16
24. 2 Chronicles 24—25; John 17
25. 2 Chronicles 26—27; John 18
26. 2 Chronicles 28—29; John 19:1-16
27. 2 Chronicles 30—31; John 19:17-42
28. 2 Chronicles 32; John 20:1-18
29. 2 Chronicles 33—34; John 20:19-31
30. 2 Chronicles 35—36; John 21

JULY

1. Ezra 1—2; Acts 1
2. Ezra 3—4; Acts 2
3. Ezra 5—6; Acts 3
4. Ezra 7—8; Acts 4:1-22
5. Ezra 9—10; Acts 4:23-37
6. Nehemiah 1—3; Acts 5
7. Nehemiah 4—6; Acts 6
8. Nehemiah 7—9; Acts 7
9. Nehemiah 10—11; Acts 8:1-25
10. Nehemiah 12—13; Acts 8:26-40
11. Esther 1—2; Acts 9:1-22
12. Esther 3—6; Acts 9:23-43
13. Esther 7—10; Acts 10:1-23
14. Job 1—3; Acts 10:24-48
15. Job 4—7; Acts 11
16. Job 8—10; Acts 12
17. Job 11—14; Acts 13:1-13
18. Job 15—17; Acts 13:14-52
19. Job 18—21; Acts 14
20. Job 22—24; Acts 15
21. Job 25—28; Acts 16:1-15
22. Job 29—31; Acts 16:16-40
23. Job 32—34; Acts 17:1-15
24. Job 35—37; Acts 17:16-34
25. Job 38—39; Acts 18
26. Job 40—42; Acts 19:1-20
27. Psalms 1—6; Acts 19:21-41
28. Psalms 7—12; Acts 20:1-16
29. Psalms 13—18; Acts 20:17-38
30. Psalms 19—24; Acts 21:1-16
31. Psalms 25—30; Acts 21:17-40

AUGUST

1. Psalms 31—36; Acts 22
2. Psalms 37—41; Acts 23
3. Psalms 42—47; Acts 24
4. Psalms 48—53; Acts 25
5. Psalms 54—58; Acts 26
6. Psalms 59—64; Acts 27
7. Psalms 65—68; Acts 28:1-15
8. Psalms 69—72; Acts 28:16-31
9. Psalms 73—77; Romans 1:1-17
10. Psalms 78—80; Romans 1:18-32
11. Psalms 81—86; Romans 2
12. Psalms 87—89; Romans 3
13. Psalms 90—95; Romans 4
14. Psalms 96—102; Romans 5
15. Psalms 103—106; Romans 6
16. Psalms 107—111; Romans 7
17. Psalms 112—118; Romans 8:1-17
18. Psalms 119:1—88; Romans 8:18-39
19. Psalms 119:89—176; Romans 9
20. Psalms 120—129; Romans 10
21. Psalms 130—136; Romans 11
22. Psalms 137—140; Romans 12
23. Psalms 141—145; Romans 13
24. Psalms 146—150; Romans 14
25. Proverbs 1—3; Romans 15
26. Proverbs 4—6; Romans 16
27. Proverbs 7—9; 1 Corinthians 1
28. Proverbs 10—12; 1 Corinthians 2
29. Proverbs 13—14; 1 Corinthians 3
30. Proverbs 15—17; 1 Corinthians 4
31. Proverbs 18—20; 1 Corinthians 5

SEPTEMBER

1. Proverbs 21—23; 1 Corinthians 6
2. Proverbs 24—26; 1 Corinthians 7
3. Proverbs 27—29; 1 Corinthians 8
4. Proverbs 30—31; 1 Corinthians 9
5. Ecclesiastes 1—3; 1 Corinthians 10
6. Ecclesiastes 4—7; 1 Corinthians 11
7. Ecclesiastes 8—12; 1 Corinthians 12
8. Song of Songs 1—4; 1 Corinthians 13
9. Song of Songs 5—8; 1 Corinthians 14
10. Isaiah 1—4; 1 Corinthians 15
11. Isaiah 5—7; 1 Corinthians 16
12. Isaiah 8—9; 2 Corinthians 1
13. Isaiah 10—12; 2 Corinthians 2
14. Isaiah 13—14; 2 Corinthians 3
15. Isaiah 15—18; 2 Corinthians 4
16. Isaiah 19—22; 2 Corinthians 5
17. Isaiah 23—25; 2 Corinthians 6
18. Isaiah 26—29; 2 Corinthians 7
19. Isaiah 30—32; 2 Corinthians 8
20. Isaiah 33—35; 2 Corinthians 9
21. Isaiah 36—39; 2 Corinthians 10
22. Isaiah 40—41; 2 Corinthians 11
23. Isaiah 42—43; 2 Corinthians 12
24. Isaiah 44—47; 2 Corinthians 13
25. Isaiah 48—50; Galatians 1
26. Isaiah 51—53; Galatians 2
27. Isaiah 54—57; Galatians 3
28. Isaiah 58—60; Galatians 4
29. Isaiah 61—63; Galatians 5
30. Isaiah 64—66; Galatians 6

HIDING GOD'S WORD IN YOUR HEART

I have hidden your word in my heart that I might not sin against you. Psalm 119:11

THE VALUE OF SCRIPTURE MEMORY

Scripture memory is an important part of the Christian life. Three reasons to memorize Scripture are:

- **Handling Difficult Situations**: A heartfelt knowledge of God's Word equips us to handle any situation that we might face. Declaring such truth as, "I can do everything through Christ" (see Philippians 4:13) and "He will never desert me nor forsake me" (see Hebrews 13:5) will enable us to walk through situations with peace and courage.

- **Overcoming Temptation**: Luke 4:1-13 describes how Jesus used Scripture to overcome His temptation in the desert. Knowledge of Scripture and the strength that comes with the ability to use it is an important part of putting on the full armor of God in preparation for spiritual warfare (see Ephesians 6:10-18).

- **Getting Guidance**: Psalm 119:105 states that the Word of God is a "lamp to my feet and a light for my path." Learn to hide God's Word in your heart so that His light can direct your decisions and actions throughout your day.

WHAT SHOULD I MEMORIZE?

Begin with the First Place memory verses. Each of these verses relates to the weekly Bible study and can help you apply the truth to your life.

Memorize Scriptures that are related to an area in your life that needs growth and truth for encouragement—prayer, forgiveness, salvation, strength, overcoming temptation, rest, worry, etc. Use a concordance to find verses on those topics that have particular meaning to you. File your verses based on these topics so that you can find them when you need them. As you read God's Word, jot down meaningful verses to add to your memory file.

THINKING ABOUT IT

Begin a list of Scripture memory verses you would like to memorize, in addition to the First Place memory verses.

➤ To help as you begin, read Proverbs 15:23; then think back to a difficult situation in the past. Can you recall a particular verse or passage of Scripture that helped pull you through or that you used to encourage someone else?

➤ Do you have the verse memorized? If so, write it here. If not, find the verse in your Bible, write it down and plan to memorize it.

➤ Think back to a time when God's Word provided a way out for you. Read 1 Corinthians 10:13. Can you recall the particular verse that helped you? Do you have this verse memorized? If so, write it here. If not, find the verse in your Bible, write it down and add it to your list of verses to be memorized.

➤ After reading Isaiah 30:21, think back to a time when a specific verse or passage of Scripture helped you discover God's will for a particular situation. Do you have this verse memorized? If so, write it here. If not, find the verse in your Bible, write it here and commit to memorizing it.

HOW TO MEMORIZE SCRIPTURE

Anyone can memorize Scripture. However, it does take a commitment of time and a willing heart. To memorize Scripture you must have a positive attitude and say with Paul, "I can do everything through him who gives me strength" (Philippians 4:13).

- Write the verse several times and read it aloud as you write it.

- Personalize the verse by putting your name in key places and say it in your own words. This will give you ownership of the verse and will help you apply it to your life.

- Seek to understand the verse by reading it in context. Study the verse and those surrounding it to understand what it means.

- To learn the reference (where the verse is found in the Bible), *glue* it to the first few words of the verse. When you say the verse, always say the reference before and after each recitation.

- Memorize the verse one phrase at a time. Dividing up the verse into its most meaningful components helps make the memorization process easier. Continue until you are able to quote the entire verse, word for word.

- Memorize Scripture with a family member or friend. Partnering with someone provides a fun component and a source of accountability.

- Try to review your verses daily for several months. Then review your verses at least once a month to keep them fresh in your mind.

- Use the First Place memory aids such as the memory verse book and the Scripture Memory CD or cassette. Keep the Scripture Memory Verse book with you to review throughout the day. Listen to the CD or cassette as you exercise or drive.

- Practice the verses while exercising or driving. Put the written verses in convenient places and recite them whenever you get the chance.

Through a lifestyle of memorizing Scripture, the Holy Spirit will be able to bring the truth to your mind in difficult times, when temptation comes or when seeking guidance for your life. God's Spirit will also bring you opportunities to share Scripture with others whether as a witness to them or to encourage them. Remember, as you hide God's Word in your heart you will truly be storing up treasures from heaven!

SHARING YOUR FAITH

But [Jesus] said to them, "I have food to eat that you know nothing about" John 4:32.

Many of the Samaritans from that town believed in [Jesus] because of the woman's testimony
John 4:39.

Nothing is more effective in drawing someone to Jesus than sharing personal life experiences. People are more open to the good news of Jesus Christ when they see faith in action. Personal faith stories are simple and effective ways to share what Christ is doing in your life because they show firsthand how Christ makes a difference.

Is your experience in First Place providing you opportunities to share with others what God is doing in your life? If you answered yes, then you have a personal faith story! If you do not have a personal faith story, perhaps it is because you don't know Jesus Christ as your personal Lord and Savior. Read through "Steps to Becoming a Christian" (pp. 29-30) and begin today to give Christ first place in your life.

Creativity and preparation in using opportunities to share a word or story about Jesus is an important part of the Christian life. Is Jesus helping you in a special way? Are you achieving a level of success or peace that you haven't experienced in other attempts to lose weight, exercise regularly or eat healthier? As people see you making changes and achieving success, they may ask you how you are doing it. How will—or do—you respond?

Remember, your story is unique and it may allow others to see what Christ is doing in your life. It may help to bring Christ into the life of another person.

PERSONAL STATEMENTS OF FAITH

First Place gives you a great opportunity to communicate to others about your faith. Look for ways to express what God is doing in your life or the lives of others. Be ready to use your own personal statement of faith whenever the opportunity presents itself.

Personal statements of faith should be short and fit naturally into a conversation. They don't require or expect any action or response from the listener. The goal is not to get another person to change but simply to help you communicate who you are and what's important to you.

Here are some examples of short statements of faith that you might use when someone asks what you are doing to lose weight:

- I've been meeting with a group at my church. We pray together, support each other, learn about nutrition and study the Bible.
- It's amazing how Bible study and prayer are helping me lose weight and eat healthier.
- I've had a lot of support from a group I meet with at church.
- I'm relying more on God to help me make changes in my lifestyle.

Begin keeping a list of your meaningful experiences as you go through First Place. Also, notice what is happening in the lives of others. Use the following questions to help you prepare short personal statements and stories of faith:

1. What is God doing in your life physically, emotionally and spiritually?

2. How has your relationship with God changed? Is it more intimate or personal? See the "Steps to Becoming a Christian" (pp. 29-30) if you have never established a relationship with Christ.

3. How is prayer, Bible study and/or the support of others helping you achieve your goals for a healthy weight and good nutrition?

DEVELOPING YOUR PERSONAL FAITH STORY

Write a brief story about how God is working in your life through First Place. Use your story to help you share with others what's happening in your life. Use the following questions to help develop your story:

➤ Briefly describe why you joined First Place. What specific circumstances led you to a Christ-centered health and weight loss program? What were you feeling when you joined?

➤ What was your relationship with Christ when you started First Place? What is it now?

➤ How has your experience in First Place changed your relationship with Christ? With yourself? With others?

➤ How has your relationship with Christ, prayer, Bible study and group support made a difference in your life?

What specific verse or passage of Scripture has made a difference in the way you view yourself or your relationship with Christ?

What experiences have impacted your life since starting First Place?

In what ways is Christ working in your life today? In what ways is He meeting your needs?

How has Christ worked in other members of your First Place group?

Summarize your answers to the above questions in a few sentences. Use your answers to help you write a short personal faith story.

STEPS TO BECOMING A CHRISTIAN

THE BIBLE SAYS

- We were made for God.
- God seeks a relationship with each of us.
- God yearns for us to spend eternity with Him in heaven.

THE BAD NEWS

Sin separates us from God and eliminates our hope for heaven. Sin is defined as missing what God wants for our lives. Think of a bull's-eye and arrows that have missed the center mark; sin means missing God's mark for us.

THE GOOD NEWS

- Jesus, God's only Son, came to Earth as a human.
- He willingly became our sacrifice by dying on the cross for our sins.
- We cannot save ourselves. Jesus' blood covers all our sins and reconciles us to God.

Have you ever made the decision to ask Jesus Christ to be your Savior? ☐ yes ☐ no

If you answered yes, on a separate sheet of paper write about your personal experience. If your answer is no, please open your heart to God now. These are the simple steps to take:

- **Acknowledge that you are a sinner.** "For all have sinned and fall short of the glory of God" (Romans 3:23).
- **Acknowledge that sin separates you from God.** "For the wages of sin is death, but the gift of God is eternal life in Christ Jesus our Lord" (Romans 6:23).
- **Acknowledge that Christ died for you.** "But God demonstrates his own love for us in this: While we were still sinners, Christ died for us" (Romans 5:8).
- **Receive Christ as Savior.** "If you confess with your mouth 'Jesus is Lord,' and believe in your heart that God raised him from the dead, you will be saved. For it is with your heart that you believe and are justified, and it is with your mouth that you confess and are saved" (Romans 10:9-10).

Now pray these words:

Dear God,
I know I am a sinner and separated from You. I believe You love me and
that You sent Jesus to die on the cross for me. I accept You as my Savior
and my Lord. Please forgive me of my sin and teach me how to give You
first place in my life. Amen.

Live-It Food Plan

RECOMMENDATIONS FOR NUTRITIONAL HEALTH

NUTRITION, HEALTH AND QUALITY OF LIFE

Dietary habits are associated with many of the leading causes of death and disability in Americans. Heart disease, cancer, stroke, diabetes, high blood pressure, obesity and osteoporosis are only a few. Experts estimate that poor dietary habits and sedentary lifestyles result in more than 300,000 deaths each year. This is second only to tobacco use as the leading cause of death and disease in this country.

Because of the importance of nutrition to health and quality of life, several leading health organizations such as the American Heart Association, the American Cancer Society, the American Diabetes Association and the United States Department of Agriculture have released dietary guidelines for Americans. These guidelines are based on hundreds of scientific studies and the consensus of leading health and nutrition experts around the world. Current guidelines represent the best available information on the role of nutrition in promoting health and well-being. The most consistent principles are that of variety, balance and moderation.

The following First Place recommendations for nutritional health are consistent with major dietary guidelines and reflect sound health and nutrition information. They are intended to enhance your health and promote effective Christian living. We recommend that you set a long-term goal of incorporating each recommendation into your Live-It plan. Set realistic goals and make gradual changes. Start with the recommendation(s) that you feel will give you the greatest benefits, and incorporate each recommendation into your lifestyle as you are ready to take the next step.

1. Eat to nourish your body and enhance your health and well being.

2. Develop a lifestyle of healthy eating that is practical, enjoyable and lifelong.

3. Achieve and maintain a healthy body weight by:

   a. Eating small portions of a variety of foods from each food group.

   b. Remembering variety, balance and moderation.

   c. Living a physically active lifestyle.

   d. Getting at least 30 minutes of moderate physical activity at least 5 days a week.

   e. Practicing healthy eating habits.

4. Eat regular meals; eat slowly; eat only when you're hungry and stop when you're comfortably full.

5. Include plenty of whole grains, fruits and vegetables in your eating plan.

6. Eat a healthy balance of lean meats, poultry, fish and low-fat dairy products.

7. Cut down on foods high in saturated fat, cholesterol, sugar and sodium.

First Place encourages an eating plan that is high in fruits, vegetables, legumes and whole grains, as well as low in fat, saturated fat and cholesterol. The plan also includes a healthy balance of lean meats, poultry, fish and low-fat dairy products, balancing calorie intake with regular physical activity to maintain a healthy body weight. A healthy eating plan limits foods high in sugar and sodium.

THE FOOD GUIDE PYRAMID

The Food Guide Pyramid, introduced in 1992 by the United States Department of Agriculture (USDA) and now adapted by most major health and nutrition organizations, offers a visual and practical way to put healthy nutrition into practice. The pyramid divides all foods into five groups based on their nutritional similarities and the number of servings needed for a healthy diet (much like exchanges). It includes an additional category for fats, oils and sweets, which should be eaten sparingly. Each food group supplies some, but not all, of the nutrients you need. No one food or food group is more important than another; you need them all for nutritional health. By eating a variety of foods from each group, sticking with the recommended number of daily servings, and putting into practice the principles of portion control, the pyramid and the Live-It plan will help you achieve your goals for healthy weight and good health.

THE FOOD GUIDE PYRAMID

For everything God created is good. 1 Timothy 4:4

Red meat and butter
Limit intake. Choose healthier alternatives

Non or low fat dairy
Milk, soymilk, yogurt, 1-2 serv/day or take a calcium supplement

Water
5-8 glasses of water daily

Legumes
Peas, beans, lentils, hummus, 1-2 serv/day (at least 3/week)

Whole grain...
Breads, cereals, and brown rice, 4-8 serv/day

Vegetables
Eat in abundance, 4-5 serv/day

Physical activity
30-60 min/day

Limit high glycemic foods
White bread, white rice, sweets, sodas, potatoes, snack foods

Multiple vitamins
May be helpful for most people

Eggs, fish, poultry, or meat alternatives
Soy burgers, tofu, gluten, 1-2 serv/day

Nuts
Almonds, walnuts, peanuts, nut butters, at least 1-2 serv/day

Plant oils
Olive, soy, and canola oil; salad dressing; avocado, 3-4 serv/day

Fruits
Oranges, bananas melons, apples, berries, 4-5 serv/day

Weight control
BMI less than 25

Daily exercise and weight control

New Food Pyramid design developed by Wellsource, Inc. © 2004. Used by permission.

FINDING YOUR HEALTHY WEIGHT

FEARFULLY AND WONDERFULLY MADE

O LORD, you have searched me and you know me. For you created me in my inmost being; you knit me together in my mother's womb. I praise you because I am fearfully and wonderfully made (Psalm 139:1,13,14).

Who has measured the waters in the hollow of his hand, or with the breadth of his hand marked off the heavens? Who has held the dust of the earth in a basket, or weighed the mountains on the scales and the hills in a balance? (Isaiah 40:12)

The latest research shows that a healthy body weight is not the popular ideal. We must break away from an unhealthy focus on thinness and physical appearance. What you weigh or how you look are not the important things to focus on; it's your relationships with God, yourself and others that count.

It's time to adopt a new perspective on weight loss. God's desire for you is to be healthy, happy and energetic. Decide today to honor and care for yourself in a manner that's pleasing to Him. Using the following worksheet, prayerfully ask God to guide you in choosing a weight and a lifestyle that's best for you. Discuss your weight and health with family, friends and your First Place group members.

1. **My Current Weight** _____
   Make sure you have an accurate measure. You will use this number to determine your weight-loss goal.

2. **My Lowest Healthy Weight After Age 21** _____
   This should be a healthy weight that you were able to maintain for at least one year. Be careful not to pick a weight that you struggled to maintain. Be honest with yourself!

3. **The Weight at Which I'll Look and Feel the Best** _____
   What weight seems most natural for you? What are the weights and body shapes of members of your family? Don't hold unrealistic expectations; consider body type and genetics in determining your goal. Your goal should be to follow a healthy and well-balanced eating plan that provides the nutrients and energy you need for enjoyable and effective living.

Women		
Height	Healthy Weight Range ± 10 lbs.	
Feet/ Inches	Low	High
4'10"	100	119
4'11"	102	124
5'0"	106	128
5'1"	110	132
5'2"	114	136
5'3"	118	141
5'4"	122	145
5'5"	125	150
5'6"	128	155
5'7"	132	159
5'8"	136	164
5'9"	140	169
5'10"	144	174
5'11"	148	179
6'0"	152	184

4. **My Recommended Healthy Weight Range** _____

   Your recommended healthy weight range is based upon the weight ranges associated with good health. A weight above the higher level places you at greater risk for future health problems such as heart disease, high blood pressure, diabetes and arthritis. The lower level represents the more popular ideal weight but is not necessary for good health and may even be unrealistic or unhealthy for you. Circle the weights listed for your height on the appropriate table. Because everyone is built a little differently, you may need to add or subtract 10 to 15 pounds from the weights listed in the table.

5. **My Healthy Weight Goal**

   - Pounds to lose _____
   - Months to goal_____

   For your healthy weight goal, select the weight you circled in the high column. If this weight seems too low for you, multiply your current weight by 0.9 to determine your healthy weight goal. Research shows that a weight loss of 10 percent results in significant health benefits. Subtract your healthy weight from your current weight to determine how many pounds you will need to lose to reach your goal. Divide the pounds you need to lose by five to determine approximately how many months it will take you to reach your goal. Losing five pounds a month is a safe and effective rate of weight loss.

Men		
Height	Healthy Weight Range ± 15 lbs.	
Feet/ Inches	Low	High
5'3"	126	141
5'4"	130	145
5'5"	135	150
5'6"	140	155
5'7"	144	159
5'8"	148	164
5'9"	153	169
5'10"	158	174
5'11"	162	179
6'0"	166	184
6'1"	170	189
6'2"	175	194
6'3"	179	200
6'4"	184	205
6'5"	189	210

6. **My Ideal Weight Goal**

   - Pounds to lose _____
   - Months to goal _____

   For your ideal weight goal, select the highest weight from numbers 2 and 3, or the weight you circled in the low column. Why the higher weight? This represents the weight that's most realistic and natural. Your goal is to reach and maintain your healthy weight. Once you achieve this goal you may want to work toward your ideal weight goal. Subtract your ideal weight from your healthy weight to determine how many pounds you will need to lose to reach your goal. Divide the pounds you need to lose by five to determine approximately how many months it will take you to reach your goal.

7. **My Personal Weight Range** : _____ to _____

   Your Personal Weight Range is between your Ideal Weight goal and your Healthy Weight goal.

Dedicate yourself and your goals to the Lord with the following prayer:

 Lord, You know me and have searched my heart. With Your help, I will reach and maintain my weight within my personal weight range. Lord, my first priority is to grow closer to You. Give me the strength, perseverance and wisdom to achieve the health and well-being You desire for me. "Thanks be to God! He gives us victory through our Lord Jesus Christ" (1 Corinthians 15:57).

CHOOSING A CALORIE LEVEL

Calories from the foods you eat provide the energy and nutrients your body needs for good health. They provide the fuel that powers your body spiritually, mentally, emotionally and physically. The key to achieving and maintaining a healthy weight lies in calorie balance. Weight gain occurs when you take in more calories than your body needs. To lose weight, you must reduce the number of calories you take in or increase the number of calories you use up.

It's best to lose weight slowly. Low-calorie diets and rapid weight loss promote a slowing of the metabolic rate, which makes it more difficult to lose and maintain your weight in the long run. Studies show that exercise may be the most important factor in the maintenance of long-term weight loss. Regular physical activity may prevent the slowing of the metabolic rate that often occurs with weight loss. Also, it's very difficult to get all the nutrients your body needs each day when your calorie intake drops too low. Because physical activity burns calories, you can take in more calories from a healthy diet and still lose weight.

Use the following tables to help you choose a daily calorie level for healthy weight loss. Choose the recommended calorie level for your age and body weight. This calorie level is your starting point for the Live-It plan.

Recommended Calorie Ranges for Women					
Age↓ / Weight→	100-119	120-139	140-159	160-179	180+
20-39	1400	1400	1500	1600	1600
40-59	1200	1400	1400	1500	1500
60+	1200	1200	1400	1400	1400

Note: *If your goal is to maintain weight, add 300-500 calories to your plan.*

Recommended Calorie Ranges for Men					
Age↓ / Weight→	140-159	160-179	180-199	200-219	220+
20-39	1800	1800	2000	2200	2400
40-59	1600	1800	1800	2000	2200
60+	1500	1600	1800	1800	2000

Note: *If your goal is to maintain weight, add 400-600 calories to your plan.*

The tables use the best available methods for estimating a calorie level for healthy weight loss; however, your needs may be different. Age, gender, heredity, body size and physical activity influence the number of calories your body needs. It's best to lose weight at a rate of one-half to two pounds each week. Adjust the calorie plan up or down based on how you feel and how well you are meeting your goals. If you are losing more than two pounds a week change to the next higher calorie level. Also, if you're not losing weight, check your portions sizes—many people don't realize how much they're eating!

A balanced diet and regular physical activity are the keys to good health and successful weight loss.

CALORIE LEVEL EXCHANGES

This daily exchange plan allow you to personalize your Live-It plan based on your nutritional needs and eating preferences. Choosing the lowest number of exchanges from each food group will give you fewer calories than listed. To stay within your calorie level, don't choose the higher number of exchanges from more than one food group. You can, however, choose the highest number of exchanges for the fruit and vegetable groups. Choose what works best for you.

Daily Exchange Plans						
Levels	Bread/Starch	Vegetable	Fruit	Meat	Milk	Fat
1200	5-6	3	2-3	4-5	2-3	3-4
1400	6-7	3-4	3-4	5-6	2-3	3-4
1500	7-8	3-4	3-4	5-6	2-3	3-4
1600	8-9	3-4	3-4	6-7	2-3	3-4
1800	10-11	3-4	3-4	6-7	2-3	4-5
2000	11-12	4-5	4-5	6-7	2-3	5-6
2200	12-13	4-5	4-5	7-8	2-3	6-7
2400	13-14	4-5	4-5	8-9	2-3	7-8
2600	14-15	5	5	9-10	2-3	7-8
2800	15-16	5	5	9-10	2-3	9-10

Note: The food exchanges break down to approximately 50-55% carbohydrate, 15-20% protein and 25-30% fat.

DESIGNING YOUR PERSONAL EATING PLAN

For your personalized eating plan, take the following steps:

- Choose your appropriate daily calorie level from the Choosing a Calorie Level table (p. 37).
- Choose your daily exchange allowance from the Daily Exchange Plan chart above.
- From your daily exchange allowance, record the total exchanges for each food group in the following My Live-It Plan.
- Distribute your daily exchange allowances into the three time periods in your plan.

See the sample plan to the right.

My Live-It Plan= *1600* calories				
	Calorie Level			
	Morning	Midday	Evening	Totals
Breads/Starches	2	3	4	9
Vegetables		1	2	3
Fruits	1	1	1	3
Meat	2	2	2	6
Milk	1	½	½	2
Fat	1	1	1	3

You may make copies of the following form for your own use:

My Live-It Plan= _____ *calories*				
	Calorie Level			
	Morning	Midday	Evening	Totals
Breads/Starches				
Vegetables				
Fruits				
Meat				
Milk				
Fat				

USING THE COMMITMENT RECORD

The Commitment Record (CR) is an aid for you in keeping track of your accomplishments. Begin a new CR on the morning of the day your class meets. This ensures that your CR is complete before your next meeting. Turn in the CR weekly to your leader. The following directions are to be used for the commitment records found in the First Place Bible studies.

CALORIE LEVEL

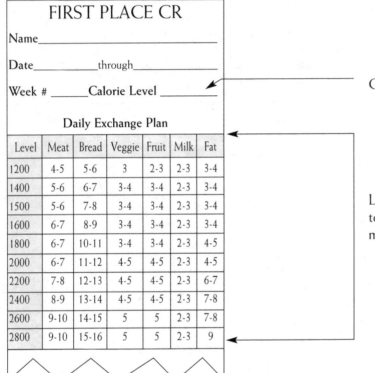

FIRST PLACE CR

Name_____

Date_____through_____

Week # _____Calorie Level _____

Daily Exchange Plan

Level	Meat	Bread	Veggie	Fruit	Milk	Fat
1200	4-5	5-6	3	2-3	2-3	3-4
1400	5-6	6-7	3-4	3-4	2-3	3-4
1500	5-6	7-8	3-4	3-4	2-3	3-4
1600	6-7	8-9	3-4	3-4	2-3	3-4
1800	6-7	10-11	3-4	3-4	2-3	4-5
2000	6-7	11-12	4-5	4-5	2-3	4-5
2200	7-8	12-13	4-5	4-5	2-3	6-7
2400	8-9	13-14	4-5	4-5	2-3	7-8
2600	9-10	14-15	5	5	2-3	7-8
2800	9-10	15-16	5	5	2-3	9

Choose your calorie level.

Limit your high-range selections to only one of the following each day: meat, bread, milk or fat.

WEEKLY PROGRESS

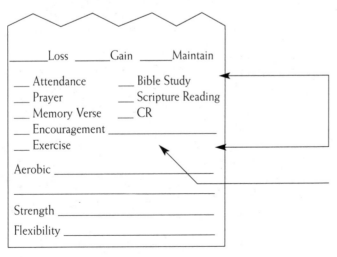

_____Loss _____Gain _____Maintain

___ Attendance ___ Bible Study
___ Prayer ___ Scripture Reading
___ Memory Verse ___ CR
___ Encouragement _____
___ Exercise

Aerobic _____

_____

Strength _____

Flexibility _____

At the end of each week, complete the weekly progress section.

Record the number of days you kept the commitment.

Write the initials of the group member you encouraged this week.

RECORDING FOOD CHOICES

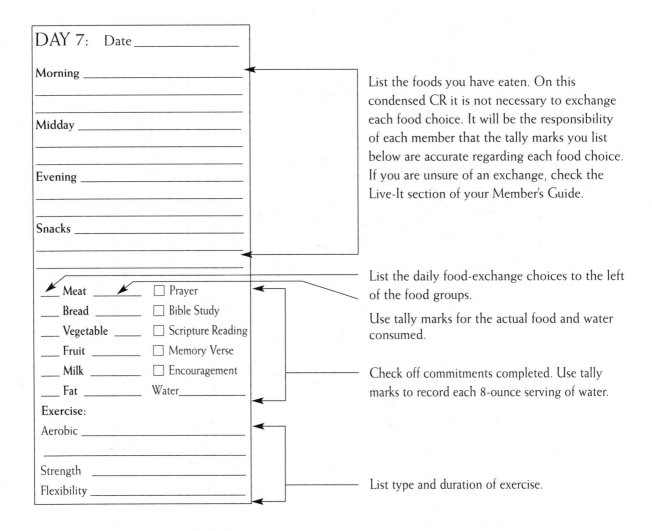

DAY 7: Date _____

Morning _____
_____
_____
Midday _____
_____
_____
Evening _____
_____
_____
Snacks _____
_____
_____

___ Meat _____   ☐ Prayer
___ Bread _____   ☐ Bible Study
___ Vegetable _____   ☐ Scripture Reading
___ Fruit _____   ☐ Memory Verse
___ Milk _____   ☐ Encouragement
___ Fat _____   Water_____
Exercise:
Aerobic _____
_____
Strength _____
Flexibility _____

List the foods you have eaten. On this condensed CR it is not necessary to exchange each food choice. It will be the responsibility of each member that the tally marks you list below are accurate regarding each food choice. If you are unsure of an exchange, check the Live-It section of your Member's Guide.

List the daily food-exchange choices to the left of the food groups.

Use tally marks for the actual food and water consumed.

Check off commitments completed. Use tally marks to record each 8-ounce serving of water.

List type and duration of exercise.

COMPLETING THE COMMITMENT RECORD

The commitment record excerpts on the following page are filled in for you, to be used as a guide. This full version of the CR can be found in the Member's Kit, and can be purchased in individually wrapped packages of 13 records each.

FIRST PLACE COMMITMENT RECORD

Name _Kay Smith_

Date _3-19-01_ through _3-25-01_

Memory Verse _Matthew 6:33_

But seek first his kingdom, and his righteousness, and all these things will be given to you as well.

Week # _3_   Calorie Level _1400_

Daily Exchanges

Meat _5-6_   Bread _6-7_   Vegetable _3-4_

Fruit _3-4_   Milk _2-3_   Fat _3-4_

Water _8_

© 2001 First Place

Weekly Progress

Weight Management

Loss _-2 lbs._   Gain _____   Maintain _____

Commitments

✓	Attendance	
7	Prayer	
7	Memory Verse	
✓	Encouragement	

_6_ Bible Study
_6_ Scripture Reading
_7_ CR
_✓_ CR / EE

Exercise   Aerobic _3 mile walk/30 minute bike ride_

Strength _15 minutes lower body_

Flexibility _____

Comments _Better week! Used CD to walk._
Took time to plan before grocery shopping.

Prayer Requests   1) _Pain in my foot_
2) _Joe's yearly check-up Wednesday_
3) _Stress with my job!_

DAY 1 / DATE _____

Morning _½ cup oatmeal = 1 bread; 1 sl. ww = 1 bread; 8 oz. skim = 1 milk; 1 tb. raisins = ½ fruit; ¼ cup apple juice in oatmeal = ½ fruit_

Midday _cheese broccoli soup = 1 mt/ ½ bd/ ½ milk/ ½ fat; 1 oz. lean ham = 1 mt; 2 sl. diet bred = 1 bred; 1 c. tomato = 1 veg; ⅛ avocado = 1 fat_

Evening _4 oz. baked fish = 4 meat; 1 t. mayo light on fish = 1 fat; ½ c. peas = 1 bred; ½ c. corn = 1 bred; ½ c. mushrms, ½ c. cooked onion = 2 veg._

Snacks _4 apricots = 1 fruit; ½ grapefruit = 1 fruit_

6	Meat	＼＼|
6	Bread	＼＼|
4	Vegetable	＼＼|
3	Fruit	|||
2	Milk	||
3	Fat	|||

✓ Prayer
✓ Bible Study
✓ Scripture Reading
✓ Memory Verse
✓ Encouragement
Water ＼＼| ///

Exercise

Aerobic _3 mile walk_

Strength _____

Flexibility _10 min. stretches_

USING THE FOOD EXCHANGES

Using food exchanges is a simple way to ensure proper nutrition. Dieticians and health professionals have used this method for many years. You can use exchanges for losing weight, gaining weight or maintaining a healthy weight. People can also use food exchanges to regain health lost by years of poor nutrition.

The phrase "food exchange" doesn't need to be intimidating. Foods are divided into seven exchange lists: bread/starch, meat, vegetable, fruit, milk, fat and free foods.

All the foods within a food list contain approximately the same amount of nutrients and calories per serving, which means that one serving of a food from the bread list may be exchanged (or substituted) for one serving of any other item in the bread list.

For example, each of the following might be one bread exchange:

- one tortilla
- one and one-half cups of puffed cereal
- one-third cup of peas

By using food exchanges in your daily eating plan, you are always able to choose foods you like that fit your lifestyle. Food exchanges:

- Encourage variety.
- Ensure well-balanced meals.
- Make menu planning easier.
- Help establish permanent lifestyle change.

Words of wisdom for those who have joined First Place to lose weight:

- There is no magic potion for losing weight.
- No gimmicks or gadgets can guarantee quick and easy weight loss.
- An effective weight-loss plan needs to be both sensible and livable.

To get long-lasting results, you will need to:

- Eat less, exercise more!
- Change behavior.
- Use portion control.
- Make sure your new habits become a permanent part of your lifestyle.

(continued)

LIVE-IT PLAN

Check out the First Place Two-Week Meal Plans in the Bible studies that include recipes and food exchanges.

The six exchange lists, or food groups, were developed to aid in menu planning for First Place. The individual diet plan prescribed by a physician and/or registered dietician indicates the number of servings from each food group that should be eaten at each meal and snack. The following chart shows the amount of nutrients and number of calories in one serving from each food group. If you cannot or choose not to eat from a particular food group, consult with a physician or nutritionist to ensure proper nutrition.

	Carbohydrates (in grams)	Protein (in grams)	Fat (in grams)	Calories
Bread/Starch	15	3	trace	80
Meat				
Lean	—	7	3	55
Medium Fat	—	7	5	75
High Fat	—	7	8	100
Vegetable	5	2	—	25
Fruit	15	—	—	60
Milk				
Fat Free	12	8	trace	90
Very Low Fat	12	8	3	105
Low Fat	12	8	5	120
Whole	12	8	8	150
Fat	—	—	5	45

BREAD/STARCH EXCHANGES

Each item on the bread/starch exchange list contains approximately **15 grams of carbohydrates, 3 grams of protein, a trace of fat and 80 calories**. The foods in this versatile list contain similar amounts of nutrients. The bread/starch list encompasses cereals, crackers, dried beans, starchy vegetables, breads and prepared foods.

	Carbohydrates (in grams)	Protein (in grams)	Fat (in grams)	Calories
Bread/Starch	15	3	trace	80

Helpful Information About Bread/Starch Exchanges

- Watch for hidden fats: 0-trace grams of fat = 1 bread
  2-3 grams of fat = 1 bread + ½ fat
  4-5 grams of fat = 1 bread + 1 fat

- Cereals equaling 80 calories count as 1 bread/starch exchange.

- Choose bread/starch products containing less than 5 grams of sugar (4 grams = 1 teaspoon of sugar). Cereal or bread containing fruit will have added grams of sugar.

- Choose products high in fiber: 25-35 grams of fiber per day is recommended.

Did You Know?

- Bread and potatoes alone are not fattening. Most of the calories come from the company they keep: sour cream, butter, gravy, etc.

- Bread/starches provide 4 calories per gram while fats provide 9 calories per gram.

- Dried beans and peas are high in fiber and protein and may be considered a meat alternative as well as a bread.

CEREALS, GRAINS AND PASTA

Barley (cooked)	⅓	cup
*Bran cereals (concentrated)	⅓	cup
*Bran cereals (flaked)	½	cup
Bulgur (cooked)	½	cup
Cooked cereals	½	cup
Couscous (cooked)	⅓	cup

HIGH-FIBER CEREALS

Grape-Nuts	3	tablespoons
Grits (cooked)	½	cup
Kasha (cooked)	½	cup
Millet (cooked)	¼	cup
Other ready-to-eat unsweetened cereals	¾	cup
Pasta (cooked)	½	cup
Puffed cereal	1 ½	cups
Rice (white or brown, cooked)	⅓	cup
Rice (wild)	½	cup
Shredded wheat	½	cup

DRIED BEANS, PEAS AND LENTILS

*Baked beans	¼	cup
*Beans and peas (cooked) such as pinto, kidney, white, split, black-eyed	⅓	cup
*Lentils (cooked)	⅓	cup

ALTERNATIVE EXCHANGE

*Beans, peas and lentils	1	cup = 2 bread + 1 lean meat
Flour, soybean	½	cup = 1bread + 2 meats + 1 fat
Miso	½	cup = 1 bread + 2 meats + 1 fat
Tempeh	½	cup = 1 bread + 2 meats + 1 fat
Wheat germ (toasted)	¼	cup = 1 bread + 1 lean meat

(continued next page)

*3 grams or more of fiber per serving.

STARCHY VEGETABLES

*Corn	½	cup
*Corn-on-the-cob (6 inches long)	1	ear
Hominy	½	cup
*Lima beans	½	cup
*Peas, green (canned or frozen)	½	cup
*Plantain	½	cup
Potato (baked)	1	small (3 ounces)
Potato (mashed)	½	cup
Pumpkin	¾	cup
Squash, winter (acorn, butternut)	¾	cup
Yam, sweet potato (plain)	⅓	cup

BREADS

Bagel	½	(1 ounce)
Bread, lite (40 calories per slice)	2	slices
Bread sticks (crisp, 4 inches x 1 ½ inch)	2	(⅔ ounce)
Croutons (low fat)	1	cup
English muffin	½	
Frankfurter or hamburger bun	½	(1 ounce)
Pita (6 inches across)	½	
Plain roll (small)	1	(1 ounce)
Raisin (unfrosted)	1	(1 ounce)
*Rye, Pumpernickel	1	(1 ounce)
Tabouli	2	tablespoons
Tortilla, corn (6 inch)	1	
Tortilla, flour (6 inch)	1 + ½ fat	
White bread (including French and Italian)	1	slice (1 ounce)
Whole-wheat bread	1	slice (1 ounce)

(continued next page)

*3 grams or more of fiber per serving.

CRACKERS AND SNACKS

Animal crackers (1 oz. low fat, low sugar)	1	bread + ½ fat
Graham crackers (2-inch square)	3	squares
Matzo	¾	ounce
Melba toast	5	slices
Oyster crackers	24	
*Popcorn (air-popped with no fat added)	3	cups
Potato chips (baked)	1	ounce
Pretzels	¾	ounce
Pudding (sugar free, made with nonfat milk)	½	bread, ½ milk
Rice cakes	2	regular, 6 mini
Rye Crisp, 2x3½ inch	4	
Saltine Crackers	6	
Tortilla chips (baked)	1	ounce
Vanilla wafers, 8 low-fat wafers	1	bread + ½ fat

BREAD PREPARED WITH FAT
Count as 1 bread/starch serving, plus 1 fat.

Biscuit (2½ inch)	1	
Chow mein noodles	½	cup
Cornbread (2 inch cube)	1	(2 ounces)
Cracker, round butter type	6	
French fried potatoes, 2-3½ inches long	10	(1½ ounces)
Hummus	¼	cup
Muffin (plain, small)	1	
Pancake (4 inch)	2	
Rolls (butter style)	1	
Stuffing, bread (prepared)	¼	cup
Taco shell, (6 inch)	1	
Tortilla chips	5	
Waffle (5x½ inch)	1	

Count these as 1 bread/starch and 2 fat exchanges.

Baking chocolate	1	ounce
Corn chips	1	ounce
Croissant	1	small (1 ounce)
Potato chips	1	ounce

(continued next page)

*3 grams or more of fiber per serving.

MISCELLANEOUS

Barbecue sauce	¼	cup
Barley (dry)	1½	tablespoons
Bran (raw, unprocessed)	½	cup
Bread crumbs (dried)	2	tablespoons
Catsup	¼	cup
Chili sauce	¼	cup
Cocoa	5	tablespoons
Cornmeal	2½	tablespoons
Cornstarch	2	tablespoons
Flour (all varieties)	1	cup = 5 bread exchanges
Malt (dry)	1	tablespoon
Tapioca	2	tablespoons
Tomato paste	6	tablespoons
Tomato sauce	1	cup
*Wheat germ	3	tablespoons
Yogurt (frozen nonfat)	3	ounces

*3 grams or more of fiber per serving.

VEGETABLE EXCHANGES

Each item on the vegetable exchange list contains **5 grams of carbohydrates and 2 grams of protein, and each exchange is 25 calories**. The generous use of assorted nutritious vegetables in your diet contributes to sound health and vitality. You may enjoy them cooked or raw.

	Carbohydrates (in grams)	Protein (in grams)	Fat (in grams)	Calories
Vegetable	5	2	—	25

Helpful Information About Vegetable Exchanges

- Eat a minimum of two vegetables a day. Three to four vegetable exchanges are encouraged.
- Fresh, frozen or canned vegetables are all good choices.
- You get more nutrition and fewer calories by munching on fresh vegetables. Keep your refrigerator well stocked with ready-to-eat vegetables.
- Prepare vegetables by grilling, steaming and stir-frying. Avoid fried vegetables.
- Any fat added during preparation must be counted.

Did You Know?

- Vegetables usually contain 2-3 grams of dietary fiber.
- Vegetables are also a good source of vitamins and minerals.
- Vegetables are naturally low in fat and sodium.
- Your salads should contain small amounts of lettuce and large amounts of raw vegetables.

VEGETABLES
Unless otherwise noted, the serving sizes for vegetables (one exchange) are: 1/2 cup cooked vegetable or vegetable juice; 1 cup of raw vegetables

Artichoke (12 medium leaves)	Asparagus
Bamboo shoots	Beans (green, wax, Italian)
Bean sprouts	Beets
Broccoli	Brussels sprouts
Cabbage (cooked)	Carrots
Carrot juice	Cauliflower
Eggplant	Greens (collard, mustard, turnip)
Heart of palm	Jicama
Kale	Kohlrabi
Leeks	Mushrooms (cooked)
Okra	Onions
Pea pods	Peppers
Pimento (3 ounces)	Rutabaga
*Sauerkraut	Shallots (4 tablespoons)
Snow peas	Spinach (cooked)
Summer squash	Tomato (one large)
*Tomato/vegetable juice	Turnips
Water chestnuts	Zucchini

*400 milligrams or more of sodium per serving.

FREE VEGETABLES: 1 cup raw

Alfalfa sprouts	Bok choy
Cabbage	Celery
Chinese cabbage	Cilantro
Cress, garden	Cucumber
Endive	Escarole
Green onion	Hot peppers
Lettuce	Mushrooms
Parsley	Radishes
Romaine	Spinach
Watercress	Zucchini

Starchy vegetables such as corn, peas and potatoes are found on the Bread/Starch exchange list.

FRUIT EXCHANGES

Each item on the fruit list contains **15 grams of carbohydrates and 60 calories**. Fruits are a wonderful addition to your food plan because of their complex carbohydrates, dietary fiber and other food components linked to good health. Also, they are readily available, taste good and are quick and easy to prepare.

	Carbohydrates (in grams)	Protein (in grams)	Fat (in grams)	Calories
Fruit	15	—	—	60

Helpful Information About Fruit Exchanges

- Most fruits have about 2 grams of fiber per serving.
- Fruits contain many important vitamins such as vitamin C.
- Fruits can be substituted for sugary desserts (fruit smoothie, fruit salad, baked apple, etc.).

Did You Know?

- You get more eating satisfaction and fewer calories by munching on fruit than by drinking fruit juices.
- You can peel and freeze overripe bananas and use later in fruit smoothies and other recipes.
- Frozen grapes make a great snack.
- The form of the food (i.e., fresh, cooked, canned, frozen, dried) will affect its fiber content.

FRUIT
Fresh, Frozen and Unsweetened Canned Fruit. Unless otherwise noted, the serving sizes for one fruit serving are: ½ cup fresh or fruit juice or ¼ cup of dried

*Apple (2 inches across, w/skin)	1 apple, 4 ounces
Applesauce (unsweetened)	½ cup
Apricots (medium, raw)	4 apricots
Apricots (canned)	½ cup, 4 halves or 4 ounces
Banana (9 inches long)	½ banana or 3 ounces
*Blackberries (raw)	¾ cup
*Blueberries (raw)	¾ cup
Boysenberries	¾ cup
Cantaloupe (5 inches)	⅓ melon or 7 ounces

*3 grams or more of fiber per serving.   (continued next page)

FRUIT

Cantaloupe cubes	1	cup
Carambola (starfruit)	3	carambola or 7½ ounces
Cherries (large, raw)	12	cherries or 3½ ounces
Cherries (canned)	½	cup
Crab apples	¾	cup or 2¾ ounces
Dewberries	¾	cup or 3 ounces
*Figs (2 inches, raw)	2	figs
Fruit cocktail (canned)	½	cup
Gooseberries	1	cup or 5 ounces
Grapefruit (medium)	½	grapefruit
Grapefruit (segments)	¾	cup
Grapes (small)	17	small
Honeydew melon (medium)	⅛	melon
Honeydew melon cubes	1	cup
Kiwi (large)	1	kiwi or 3¼ ounces
Mandarin oranges	¾	cup
Mango (small)	½	mango or 3 ounces
Mulberries	1	cup or 5 ounces
*Nectarine (1½)	1	nectarine or 5 ounces
Orange (2½)	1	orange or 6½ ounces
Papaya	1	cup or 8 ounces
Passion fruit	4	passion fruit or 4 ounces
Peach (2¾)	1	peach or ¾ cup
Peaches (canned)	½	cup or 2 halves
*Pear w/skin	½	large or 1 small
Pear (canned)	½	cup or 2 halves
Persimmon (medium)	2	persimmons
Pineapple (raw)	¾	cup
Pineapple (canned)	⅓	cup
Plums	2	small or 5 ounces
*Pomegranate, raw	½	medium
*Raspberries	1	cup
Rhubarb (diced)	2	cups
*Strawberries (raw)	1¼	cups
*Strawberries (frozen)	1	cup
Tangelos	1	medium
Tangerines	2	small, 8 ounces
Watermelon	1	slice or 13½ ounces
Watermelon cubes	1¼	cups

*3 grams or more of fiber per serving.

(continued next page)

DRIED FRUIT

*Apples	4	rings or ¾ ounce
*Apricots	7	halves or ¾ ounce
Dates	2½	medium
*Figs	1½	
Prunes	3	medium or 1 ounce
Raisins	2	tablespoons or ¾ ounce

FRUIT JUICE

Apple juice/cider, grapefruit, orange, pineapple juices and most nectars	½	cup
Cranberry, grape and prune juices	⅓	cup
Lemon or lime juices	1	cup
Orange juice concentrate	2	tablespoons or 1 ounce

*3 grams or more of fiber per serving.

MEAT EXCHANGES

Each item on the meat exchange list contains approximately **7 grams of protein, some fat and no carbohydrates**. The meat exchange is divided into three groups according to how much fat it contains:

	Carbohydrates (in grams)	Protein (in grams)	Fat (in grams)	Calories
Meat				
Lean	—	7	3	55
Medium Fat	—	7	5	75
High Fat	—	7	8	100

- Lean meats have 55 calories per ounce (0-3 grams of fat).
- Medium-fat meats have 75 calories per ounce (5 grams of fat).
- High-fat meats have 100 calories per ounce (8 grams of fat).

Helpful Information About Meat Exchanges

- Most exchanges are based on one-ounce servings of cooked meat.
- Broil, bake or grill without adding fats when preparing meats. Remove all visible fat.
- Add 1 extra fat exchange per ounce to any fried meat.
- Leave skin on poultry when roasting, but remove it before eating.

Did You Know?

- The palm of your hand or a deck of cards is the same size as three ounces of meat.
- Limiting high fat meats will lower your consumption of saturated fats.
- Meats provide a generous amount of protein, the nutrient responsible for tissue building and repair.
- Most food on the lean-meat list is low in cholesterol and saturated fat.
- Beans, peas, soy products and eggs can be used as alternates to meat, poultry and fish.

LEAN MEAT AND SUBSTITUTES
(Fewer than 3 grams of fat) Count as 1 meat exchange.

Beef	Top round, boneless sirloin, flank steak, pot roast, sirloin tip roast, tenderloin, lean ground beef, London broil, strip steak, breakfast steak, filet mignon	1	ounce
Pork	Lean pork, such as fresh ham; canned, cured or boiled ham; *Canadian bacon; *tenderloin	1	ounce
Veal	All cuts are lean except for veal cutlets (ground or cubed)	1	ounce
Poultry	Chicken, turkey, Cornish hen (without skin)	1	ounce
Fish	Catfish, haddock, halibut, herring, orange roughy, trout, salmon (not canned), sole or * tuna in water ($\frac{1}{4}$ cup)	1	ounce
Shellfish	*Clams, crab, lobster, scallops and shrimp	2	ounces
Game	Venison, rabbit	1	ounce
Cheese	Any cottage cheese	$\frac{1}{4}$	cup
	Grated parmesan	2	tablespoons
	*Fat-free cream cheese	2	ounces
	*Fat-free cheese	1	ounce
Other	Fat-free luncheon meat	1	ounce
	Egg whites	3	
	Egg substitutes	$\frac{1}{4}$	cup
	Frankfurter (up to 3 grams fat/ounce)	1	ounce

*400 milligrams or more of sodium per serving.

ALTERNATIVE EXCHANGE

**Beans, peas, lentils	1	cup =
	2	bread +
	1	meat

**3 grams or more of fiber per serving.

MEDIUM-FAT MEAT AND SUBSTITUTES
(Fewer than 5 grams of fat) Count as 1 meat + ½ fat.

Beef	Ground beef, roast (rib, chuck, rump) and steak (cubed, Porterhouse, T-bone)	1 ounce
Pork	Chops, loin roast, Boston butts and cutlets	1 ounce
Lamb	Chops, leg and roast	1 ounce
Veal	Cutlet (ground or cubed, not breaded)	1 ounce
Poultry	Chicken (with skin), domestic duck or goose (with fat well drained) and ground turkey	1 ounce
	Turkey bacon	2 slices
Fish	*Tuna (canned in oil, drained),*canned salmon	¼ cup
Cheese	Light, skim or part-skim milk cheeses (i.e. mozzarella)	1 ounce
	Ricotta	¼ cup
Other	*Luncheon meat	1 ounce
	Egg	1
	Tofu	4 ounces
	Frankfurter (up to 5 grams fat/ounce)	1 ounce
	Liver, heart, kidney, sweetbreads (high in cholesterol)	1 ounce

HIGH-FAT MEAT AND SUBSTITUTES
(Fewer than 8 grams of fat) Count as 1 meat + 1 fat.
THE FOLLOWING ARE HIGH IN FAT AND SHOULD BE USED SPARINGLY.

Beef	USDA prime cuts of beef such as ribs, brisket and *corned beef	1 ounce
Pork	Spareribs, ground pork, *pork sausage (patty or link)	1 ounce
Lamb	Patties (ground lamb)	
Cheese	All regular cheeses, such as American, bleu, cheddar, Colby, Monterey Jack, Swiss	1 ounce
Other	*Luncheon meats, such as bologna, salami, pimento loaf	1 ounce
	* Sausage, knockwurst, *bratwurst	1 ounce
	Frankfurter (up to 8 grams of fat/ounce)	1 ounce
	Peanut butter (unsaturated fat)	1 tablespoon

*400 milligrams or more of sodium per serving.

MILK EXCHANGES

Each item on the milk exchange list contains **12 grams of carbohydrates, 8 grams of protein, and 90 calories.** Fat content and calories vary depending on the product you use. As a general rule, milk exchanges can be divided into four main categories:

	Carbohydrates (in grams)	Protein (in grams)	Fat (in grams)	Calories
Milk				
Fat Free	12	8	trace	90
Very Low Fat	12	8	3	105
Low Fat	12	8	5	120
Whole	12	8	8	150

- Fat free: 0 grams of fat per exchange

- Very low fat: under 3 grams of fat per exchange

- Low fat: 5 grams of fat per exchange

- Whole: 8 grams of fat per exchange

Milk exchanges are the body's main source of calcium, the mineral needed for growth and repair of bones. It is important to consume at least two milk exchanges daily.

Helpful Information About Milk Exchanges

- Many tasty dishes, including smoothies and sugar-free pudding, can be made with milk. Try the many different recipes in your cookbook.

- If you are used to whole-milk products, you may find it easier to make the change slowly to lower-fat foods. Try 2% milk first. When you're used to that, move to 1% milk. Your transition will be much easier if you later decide to change to fat-free/nonfat milk.

- **Note:** Grams of sugar appearing on the label of sugar-free dairy products is not added sugar and should be ignored.

- Any dairy yogurt containing 100 calories or less per serving is one milk exchange.

- Frozen yogurt is found on the bread/starch exchange list.

Did You Know?

- Milk has more protein per exchange than meat.

- Fat-free, ½% and 1% fat milk all provide the same nutrients as whole milk and 2% fat milk. But they are much lower in fat, saturated fatty acids, cholesterol and calories.

Are You Lactose Intolerant?

- Drink milk in smaller amounts (i.e., ½ cup or less at a time).
- Use yogurt that contains live and active cultures instead of regular milk.
- Drink lactose-reduced milk.
- Add lactase drops to milk or use lactase pills.

FAT-FREE MILK PRODUCTS
One Exchange = 1 Milk

Fat-free milk or ½ % milk	1	cup
Fat-free buttermilk	1	cup
Evaporated skim milk	½	cup
Dry nonfat milk	¼	cup
Dairy yogurt (fat free, sugar free)	8	ounces
Lactaid	1	cup

VERY LOW-FAT MILK PRODUCTS
One Exchange = 1 milk + ½ fat

1% milk	1	cup

LOW-FAT MILK PRODUCTS
One Exchange = 1 milk + 1 fat

1½ % milk or 2% milk	1	cup
Plain yogurt (low fat, sugar free)	8	ounces

WHOLE MILK
One Exchange = 1 milk + 2 fat
(Try to limit your choices from the whole milk group as much as possible.)

Whole milk	1	cup
Evaporated whole milk	½	cup
Plain whole sugar-free yogurt	8	ounces

MISCELLANEOUS

Hot chocolate (sugar free)	1	packet = ½ milk
Pudding, (sugar free, prepared with fat-free milk)	½	cup = ½ milk, ½ bread
Dairy shake (sugar free)	1	packet = 1 milk

CHEESE, OPTIONAL MILK EXCHANGE

Cottage cheese	½	cup
Cheese	2	ounces

*Choose cheese high in calcium and other nutrients you expect to get from a milk exchange. Fat grams will count as a fat exchange.

FAT EXCHANGES

Each item on the fat exchange list contains **5 grams of fat and 45 calories**. The Live-It plan limits your fat intake to 25 percent of your daily calorie total. One-half of your fat allotment comes from your lean meat choices. The other half is chosen from the fat exchange list.

	Carbohydrates (in grams)	Protein (in grams)	Fat (in grams)	Calories
Fat	—	—	5	45

Helpful Information About Fat Exchanges

→ Saturated fat is found in meat and dairy products. Choose polyunsaturated and monounsaturated fats when possible for this exchange.

→ Check labels carefully to find hidden fat.

→ Use less added fat, and use spray-on vegetable coatings instead of oils to fry or cook foods.

→ Add flavor to low-fat foods by using spices and marinating with nonfat dressings.

Did You Know?

1. You should not eliminate fat completely from your meal plan because it is necessary to
   → Provide energy.
   → Help in the transport and storage of important vitamins.
   → Build substances such as hormones that help the body work.
   → Keep us satisfied by slowing the rate of digestion.
   → Provide pleasurable taste and texture to foods.
   → Allow the gall bladder to function properly

2. The risks associated with eating too much fat are:
   → Heart disease   → Stroke
   → Certain cancers   → Diabetes
   → Gall bladder disease   → High blood pressure

3. Gram for gram, fat supplies more than twice the amount of calories in either carbohydrates or protein.
   → 1 gram protein = 4 calories
   → 1 gram carbohydrates = 4 calories
   → 1 gram fat = 9 calories

UNSATURATED FATS

Almond butter	1	teaspoon
Avocado	⅛	medium
Margarine	1	teaspoon
Margarine (lite)	1	tablespoon
Mayonnaise	1	teaspoon
Mayonnaise (lite)	1	tablespoon
Peanut butter	1	teaspoon
Nuts and seeds:		
Almonds (dry roasted)	6	whole
Cashews (dry roasted)	1	tablespoon
Chopped nuts	1	tablespoon
Peanuts	20	small or 10 large
Pecans	2	whole
Pumpkin seeds	2	teaspoons
Seeds, pinenuts, sunflower (without shells)	1	tablespoon
Walnuts	2	whole
Oil (corn, cottonseed, safflower, soybean, sunflower, olive, peanut)	1	teaspoon
Olives	10	small or 5 large
*Salad Dressing (regular)	1	teaspoon
*Salad Dressing (lite)	1	tablespoon

SATURATED FATS—NOT RECOMMENDED!

Bacon (cooked)	1	slice
Bacon grease	1	teaspoon
Butter	1	teaspoon
Butter (reduced fat)	1	tablespoon
Cheese spread	1	tablespoon
Chicken fat	1	teaspoon
Chitterlings	½	ounce
Chocolate (unsweetened)	1	ounce = 1 bread + 2 fats
Coconut (shredded)	2	tablespoons
*Coffee whitener (liquid)	2	tablespoons
*Coffee whitener (powder)	4	teaspoons
Cream cheese	1	tablespoon
Cream cheese (lite)	2	tablespoons
Cream (half-and-half)	2	tablespoons
Gravy	¼	cup
*Gravy (packaged)	½	cup
Lard	1	teaspoon

(continued next page)

*Read label: 5 grams fat =1 fat exchange.

SATURATED FATS

Meat fat	1	teaspoon
Salt pork	¼	ounce
Shortening	1	teaspoon
Sour cream	2	tablespoons
Sour cream (light)	3	tablespoons
Whipping cream	1	tablespoon
*Whipped topping	3	tablespoons

*Read label: 5 grams fat = 1 fat exchange

FREE FOODS

The items on the free foods exchange list are foods very low in nutritional value and usually low in calories. Limit the total number of calories from this exchange to 50 per day.

Helpful Information About Free Foods

- Many of the foods or drinks listed contain sugar substitutes. First Place recommends using these in moderation only.
- Use these free foods to add the gourmet touches that make your meals as pleasant and attractive to serve as they are to eat.
- Check each label for serving size and caloric value.
- Measure free foods carefully. Calories add up fast!
- Free foods are not listed on your Commitment Record.

Did You Know?

- Butter spray is a nice complement to bread, baked potato, corn-on-the-cob, popcorn and vegetables.
- All fat-free dressings are on this list, but may contain high amounts of sugar. Check labels.
- When eating small amounts of food, such as one tablespoon of fat-free cream cheese on a bagel, count the cream cheese in your free food totals.

FREE FOODS

DRINKS	SNACKS
Bouillon or broth without fat	Candies (sugar free)
Carbonated drinks (sugar free)	Chewing gum (sugar free)
Carbonated water	Frozen novelty bar (sugar free)
Club soda	Gelatin (sugar free)
Coffee/tea	Pickles (unsweetened)
Drink mixes (sugar free)	
Iced Tea (sugar free)	
Tonic Water	

(continued next page)

CONDIMENTS

Bacon bits (imitation)

Barbecue sauce

Butter flavoring (powdered)

Catsup

Chili sauce

Cocktail sauce

Cocoa powder (unsweetened)

Chocolate milk mix (sugar free)

Coffee whiteners (nondairy)

Cooking spray

Enchilada sauce

Fruit spreads (sugar free)

Horseradish

Lemon or lime juice

Mayonnaise (fat free)

Mustard

Picante sauce

Pickle relish

Salad dressings (fat free)

Salsa

Salt (seasoned)

Sour cream (fat free)

Soy sauce

Steak sauce

Sugar substitutes

Syrup (sugar-free)

Tabasco sauce

Taco sauce

Teriyaki sauce

Tomato sauce

Vinegar

Whipped topping (fat free)

Worcestershire sauce

WATER

- For good health, drink at least eight 8-ounce glasses of water a day. For every 25 pounds over your healthy weight, add an additional 8 ounces of water.

- Thirst is not always the best indication of the body's need for water. By the time you're thirsty, it is often too late. Plan to drink water regularly.

- Adequate water is necessary to burn fat.

- Water helps to maintain proper muscle tone by giving muscles their natural ability to contract. It also helps to prevent sagging skin.

- Water can help relieve constipation.

- If eight glasses of water seems impossible, start where you can and increase as you can until you reach recommended amount.

LIVE-IT: THE VEGETARIAN WAY

Most experts now agree that a well-planned vegetarian eating program can supply all the nutrients your body needs for good health. In fact, research shows that eating the vegetarian way can reduce the risk for many health problems such as coronary heart disease, high blood pressure, diabetes and some forms of cancer. Of course, any eating plan that's well balanced and includes a variety of foods can lower your risk for disease and improve your overall health and quality of life. While verses such as the following clearly reveal that eating meat is appropriate, a vegetarian lifestyle can also be a healthy choice when well planned.

- "Everything that lives and moves will be food for you. Just as I gave you the green plants, I now give you everything" (Genesis 9:3).
- "He who eats meat, eats to the Lord, for he gives thanks to God; and he who abstains, does so to the Lord and gives thanks to God" (Romans 14:6).
- "Everything God created is good" (1 Timothy 4:4).

What Is a Vegetarian Diet?
Several different vegetarian eating plans exist. Here's a list of the most common:

- **Vegans** are strict vegetarians who eat only plant foods such as fruits, vegetables, legumes (dried beans and peas), grains, seeds and nuts.
- **Lacto-vegetarians** include cheese and other dairy products in their diet.
- **Lacto-ovo vegetarians** include both eggs and dairy products.
- **Semivegetarians** exclude red meat, but occasionally include poultry and fish.

Healthy Vegetarian Eating

- A properly planned vegetarian diet includes adequate amounts of protein, calories, vitamins and minerals, and is low in saturated fat, total fat and cholesterol.

- Eat a variety of foods, including whole grains, vegetables, fruits, legumes, nuts, seeds and low fat dairy products and eggs, if desired. Limit eggs to three yolks per week.

- Limit fats, oils and sweets.

- If you desire, eat up to three servings of milk, yogurt and cheese daily. Choose low fat or nonfat varieties of these foods.

- Eat two to three servings daily of legumes, nuts, seeds, peanut butter, eggs and tofu.

The following foods and servings count as one meat exchange each:

- 1 cup soy milk (choose products fortified with calcium, vitamin D and vitamin B_{12}.)
- 1 cup cooked dry or canned beans or peas
- 1 egg or 3 egg whites (limit to three egg yolks per week)
- 2 tablespoons nuts or seeds
- $\frac{1}{4}$ to $\frac{1}{2}$ cup tofu, soy cheese or tempeh
- 1 tablespoon peanut or other nut butters

➤ Eat four or more servings of vegetables daily.

➤ Eat three or more servings of fruit daily.

➤ Eat six or more servings of the bread/starch exchange daily.

Following the above plan should ensure that you get adequate amounts of protein, calories, iron, calcium, vitamin B_{12}, vitamin D and zinc, particularly if you eat dairy products and eggs. It's important to know, however, that eating vegetarian doesn't necessarily mean eating low fat. Many meat alternatives such as dairy products can be higher in fat and calories than meat.

It may be necessary to combine specific foods during a meal to obtain a complete protein. Animal proteins are considered complete proteins because they supply all the essential amino acids your body needs, while many plant-based proteins come up short in one or two.

Helpful Tips

➤ Use meat alternatives such as legumes or tofu in casseroles, stir fry, chili and other meat dishes.

➤ Try substituting tofu, soy cheese, or soy or rice milk for dairy products such as milk, cheese and yogurt. Use only products that are calcium fortified.

➤ Add rice, pasta, barley, tabouli and other grains to soups, stew, chili and other dishes.

➤ Choose vitamin fortified breakfast cereals.

➤ Enjoy a variety of fresh, frozen, canned and dried fruits and vegetables every day.

➤ Add extra vegetables to pasta dishes, soups, salads and casseroles.

➤ Add beans, peas, other legumes, nuts and seeds to salads to boost the protein content.

➤ Choose restaurants that offer a variety of vegetarian dishes. Ethnic restaurants, such as Asian and Indian, offer a variety of tasty vegetarian dishes.

➤ Many meat alternatives, such as cheese and nuts, are very high in fat and calories.

➤ Order salads, soups, breads and fruits if a restaurant doesn't offer vegetarian dishes.

➤ When traveling, call the airline at least 48 hours in advance to ask for a vegetarian meal.

EATING ON THE GO

Have you ever found yourself at the end of the day tired, hungry and having less than an hour to eat? Fortunately fast-food restaurants provide more healthy choices than ever before. What choices can you make that fit the Live-It plan?

Helpful Information About Eating Out

- Decide beforehand what you plan to eat; and if you're with others, place your order first so you won't be tempted to stray from your healthy eating plan.

- Remember portion control. Order small sizes in food selections.

- Order hamburgers and sandwiches dry, with condiments on the side.

- Chicken or fish should be grilled dry.

- Visuals help when estimating portion sizes:
    - A pancake should be the size of a compact disc.
    - A 3-ounce portion of meat should be the size of a cassette tape.
    - A ½ cup serving of mashed potatoes or pasta should be the size of a tennis ball.

- Most good choices have been listed in the fast-food guide on the following pages.

Did You Know?

- Fast-food restaurants do have healthy choices!

- Fast-food restaurants offer little or no fruit or vegetables. Make sure you get enough of these at home.

- Cheese added to sandwiches/hamburgers adds 1 meat and 1 fat per slice or ounce.

- You can order pizza with less cheese, extra vegetables and lean meats such as Canadian bacon.

- Low-fat and nonfat salad dressings are almost always available.

- Creamy salads (potato, macaroni or other pastas) are high in fat.

The following pages give suggested lower-fat food and exchanges from some fast food restaurants. If you want a more detailed account of the food they offer see *Fast Food Facts* by Marion J. Franz. You can also check the individual websites for the latest nutrition information; the addresses are listed beside each name.

FOOD ITEM	EXCHANGES

BURGER KING (www.burgerking.com)

BK Broiler chicken (without sauce)	3 bread, 3 meat, 1 fat
Hamburger	2 bread, 2 meat, 2 fat
Chicken Tenders (8 pieces)	1 bread, 3 meat, 1 ½ fat
Broiled chicken salad (dry)	2 vegetable, 3 meat
Garden salad (dry)	1 vegetable, ½ meat, 1 fat
Side salad (dry)	1 vegetable, ½ meat, ½ fat
Italian salad dressing (fat-free, 1 ounce)	free
Orange juice	2 fruit

CHICK-FIL-A (www.chickfila.com)
Most of the sandwiches at Chick-fil-A are very low in fat.

Chargrilled chicken deluxe sandwich	2 bread, 3 meat
Chick-fil-A Chicken Sandwich	2 ½ bread, 3 meat, 1 fat
Chick-fil-A Chick-n-Strips (4 oz.)	1 bread, 4 meat
Waffle Potato Fries	3 bread, 2 fat
Hearty breast of chicken soup	½ bread, 1 lean meat
Carrot & raisin salad (small)	2 vegetable, 1 fruit
Chargrilled chicken garden salad	1 vegetable, 4 lean meat
Diet lemonade	free
Chicken salad plate	2 bread, 3 meat
Chick-n-Strips Salad	1 bread, 4 ½ meat, 1 fat
Ice cream (small cone)	1 bread, 1 fat

DAIRY QUEEN (www.dairyqueen.com)

Chicken breast fillet sandwich	2 ½ bread, 3 meat, 1 ½ fat
DQ Homestyle Hamburger	2 bread, 2 meat, 1 fat
Grilled chicken breast fillet sandwich	2 bread, 3 meat
DQ fudge bar	1 bread
DQ vanilla orange bar	1 bread

Domino's Pizza (www.dominos.com)

Salads	1 vegetable
Cheese, hand tossed (2 slices of 14 inch)	3 bread, 1 meat, ½ fat
Cheese, thin (⅙ of 14 inch)	2 bread, 1 meat, 1½ fat
Toppings per slice:	
Ham	free
Vegetables	free
Pineapple	free

Jack in the Box (www.jackinthebox.com)

Chicken Fajita Pita	1½ bread, 3 meat
Hamburger	2 bread, 1½ meat, ¾ fat
Chicken breast pieces (5)	1½ bread, 3 meat, 2 fat
Garden chicken salad	1 vegetable, 3 meat
Side salad	1 vegetable
Italian salad dressing (low calorie)	free
Breakfast Jack	2 bread, 2 meat, 1 fat

KFC (www.kfc.com)

Tender Roast without skin	
Breast	4½ meat
Drumstick	1½ meat
Thigh	2 lean meat
Original or hot and spicy drumstick	½ bread, 2 meat, 1 fat
Crispy strips	½ bread, 3 meat, 1½ fat
BBQ-Flavored chicken sandwich	2 bread, 2 meat
BBQ baked beans	2 bread, ½ fat
Corn-on-the-cob	2 bread, ½ fat
Green beans	1 vegetable
Garden rice (single serving)	1½ bread
Mashed potatoes and gravy (single serving)	1 bread, 1 fat
Macaroni and cheese (single serving)	1½ bread, 1 fat

Little Caesar's (www.littlecaesars.com)

Pan!Pan! Cheese Pizza (medium, 1 slice)	1½ bread, 1 meat, ½ fat
Pan!Pan! Pepperoni Pizza	1½ bread, 1 meat, 1 fat
Crazy Bread (1 slice)	1 bread, ½ fat
Caesar salad (no dressing)	3 vegetable, 1 meat, ½ fat
Crazy Sauce (1 packet)	1 bread
Tossed Salad	3 vegetable, ½ fat
Italian salad dressing (fat free)	free

LONG JOHN SILVERS (www.longjohnsilvers.com)

FlavorBaked Chicken (no sauce)	2½	meat
FlavorBaked Fish	2	meat
Batter dipped fish sandwich (no sauce)	2	bread, 2 meat, 1 fat
FlavorBaked Chicken Sandwich (no sauce)	2	bread, 2½ meat
Plain baked potato	3	bread
Green beans	1	vegetable
Side salad	1	vegetable
Rice pilaf (single serving)	2	bread
Corn cobette (without butter)	1	bread
Cole slaw (single serving)	1	bread, 1 fat

McDONALD'S (www.mcdonalds.com)

Grilled Chicken Deluxe (plain, no sauce)	2½	bread, 3 meat
Hamburger	2	bread, 1½ meat, ¾ fat
Quarter Pounder	2½	bread, 3 meat, 1½ fat
Garden salad	1	vegetable
Grilled chicken deluxe salad	1	vegetable, 3 meat
Herb vinaigrette salad dressing (fat free, 1 packet)	½	bread
Orange juice	2	fruit
Egg McMuffin	2	bread, 2 meat, 1 fat
Hash browns	1	bread, 1 fat
Scrambled eggs	2	meat, 1 fat
English muffin (dry)	2	bread
Hotcakes (plain)	3½	bread, 1 fat
Ice cream cone (low fat)	½	milk, ½ bread, 1 fat
Chef Shaker Salad	2½	lean meat, 1 vegetable
Garden Shaker Salad	1	med.-fat meat, 1 vegetable
Grilled chicken Caesar salad	1½	very lean meat, 1 vegetable
FF Herb vinaigrette dressing	½	bread
Honey mustard dressing	1	bread, 2 fat
Ranch dressing	4	fat
Red French reduced-fat dressing	1	bread, 1 fat
Thousand Island dressing	1	bread, 2 fat

PIZZA HUT (www.pizzahut.com)
Add toppings and use Live-It Plan to calculate.

Thin and Crispy cheese (slice)	1½	bread, 1 meat, 1½ fat
Hand Tossed, cheese (1 slice)	2	bread, 2 meat, 1 fat
Veggie Lovers		
Thin and crispy (1 slice)	1½	bread, 1 meat, ½ fat
Hand-tossed pizza (1 med.)	2	bread, 1 meat, ½ fat

SUBWAY (www.subway.com)
6-inch sandwiches, no oil or mayo

Cold Cut Trio sub	3	bread, 2 meat, 1 fat
Ham or roast beef sub	3	bread, 2 meat
Turkey breast sub	3	bread, 2 meat
Meatball sub	3 ½	bread, 2 meat, 1 fat
Roasted chicken breast sub	3	bread, 3 meat
Steak and cheese sub	3	bread, 3 meat
Subway Melt sub	3	bread, 2 meat, 1 fat
Veggie Delite	3	bread
Salads without dressings		
Ham salad	2	vegetable, 1 meat
Roast Beef salad	2	vegetable, 1 meat
Roasted chicken breast salad	3	vegetable, 1 meat
Subway club salad	2	vegetable, 2 meat
Turkey breast salad	2	vegetable, 1 meat
Salad dressings (fat free)		
French	free	
Italian	free	

TACO BELL (www.tacobell.com)

Steak soft taco	1	bread, 2 meat
Pintos and cheese	½	bread, 1 meat, 1 ½ fat
Chicken soft taco	1 ½	bread, 1 ½ meat
Bean burrito	3	bread, 1 meat, 1 ½ fat

TCBY (www.tcby.com)
Use sugar-free toppings and real fruit to make a sundae.

Yogurt (no sugar added, nonfat, ½ cup)	1	bread
Yogurt (nonfat ½ cup)	1 ½	bread

WENDY'S (www.wendys.com)

Grilled chicken sandwich	2	bread, 3 meat
Junior hamburger	2	bread, 1 meat, ½ fat
Single hamburger (plain)	2	bread, 3 meat, 1 ½ fat
Garden ranch chicken pita	3	bread, 4 meat
Baked potato (plain)	4	bread
Baked potato, sour cream and chives	4 ½	bread, 1 fat
Chili, small	1	bread, 2 meat, 1 fat
Caesar side salad (without dressing)	1	vegetable, 1 meat, ½ fat
Grilled chicken salad	2	vegetable, 3 meat
Side salad	1	vegetable

FIRST PLACE GROCERY LIST

Use this list to get you started and make copies so that you will have a list for each week.

BAKING GOODS

- ☐ _____ Baking soda
- ☐ _____ Baking powder
- ☐ _____ Cocoa
- ☐ _____ Cornstarch
- ☐ _____ Dried herbs
- ☐ _____ Nuts
- ☐ _____ Pepper
- ☐ _____ Raisins
- ☐ _____ Salt
- ☐ _____ Spices
- ☐ _____ Vanilla
- ☐ _____ _____
- ☐ _____ _____
- ☐ _____ _____
- ☐ _____ _____

BEVERAGES

- ☐ _____ Cocoa
- ☐ _____ Coffee
- ☐ _____ Fruit juice, 100%
- ☐ _____ Mineral water
- ☐ _____ Soft drinks, diet
- ☐ _____ Tea
- ☐ _____ _____
- ☐ _____ _____
- ☐ _____ _____
- ☐ _____ _____

BREADS

- ☐ _____ Bagels
- ☐ _____ Breads
- ☐ _____ Buns
- ☐ _____ English muffins
- ☐ _____ Rolls
- ☐ _____ _____
- ☐ _____ _____
- ☐ _____ _____
- ☐ _____ _____

CANNED GOODS

- ☐ _____ Applesauce
- ☐ _____ Beans
- ☐ _____ Chili
- ☐ _____ Fruit
- ☐ _____ Mushrooms

- ☐ _____ Soup
- ☐ _____ Spaghetti sauce
- ☐ _____ Stewed tomatoes
- ☐ _____ Tomato paste
- ☐ _____ Tomato sauce
- ☐ _____ Tuna/salmon
- ☐ _____ Vegetables
- ☐ _____ _____
- ☐ _____ _____
- ☐ _____ _____
- ☐ _____ _____

CONDIMENTS

- ☐ _____ All-fruit/jam/jelly
- ☐ _____ Honey
- ☐ _____ Ketchup
- ☐ _____ Low-fat mayonnaise
- ☐ _____ Mustard
- ☐ _____ Olive oil
- ☐ _____ Olives
- ☐ _____ Peanut butter
- ☐ _____ Pickles
- ☐ _____ Relish
- ☐ _____ Salad dressings
- ☐ _____ Salsa
- ☐ _____ Soy sauce
- ☐ _____ Syrup, diet
- ☐ _____ Vegetable oil
- ☐ _____ Vinegar

DAIRY

- ☐ _____ Butter, reduced fat
- ☐ _____ Cream cheese
- ☐ _____ Cottage cheese
- ☐ _____ Eggs/egg sub.
- ☐ _____ Low-fat margarine
- ☐ _____ Low-fat sour cream
- ☐ _____ Milk, fat free/1%
- ☐ _____ Other cheese
- ☐ _____ Parmesan cheese
- ☐ _____ Yogurt (90-calorie)
- ☐ _____ _____
- ☐ _____ _____
- ☐ _____ _____
- ☐ _____ _____

DRY GOODS

- ☐ _____ Beans/peas/lentils
- ☐ _____ Bread crumbs
- ☐ _____ Cereals
- ☐ _____ Cornmeal
- ☐ _____ Crackers
- ☐ _____ Flour
- ☐ _____ Oatmeal
- ☐ _____ Pancake mix
- ☐ _____ Pasta/noodles
- ☐ _____ Rice
- ☐ _____ Sugar/sugar sub.
- ☐ _____ Sugar-free pudding
- ☐ _____ Tortilla chips
- ☐ _____ _____
- ☐ _____ _____
- ☐ _____ _____
- ☐ _____ _____

FROZEN FOODS

- ☐ _____ Frozen dinners
- ☐ _____ Frozen waffles
- ☐ _____ Light whipped topping
- ☐ _____ Light yogurt/ ice cream
- ☐ _____ Vegetables
- ☐ _____ _____
- ☐ _____ _____
- ☐ _____ _____
- ☐ _____ _____

FRUIT

- ☐ _____ Apples
- ☐ _____ Bananas
- ☐ _____ Berries
- ☐ _____ Grapefruit
- ☐ _____ Grapes
- ☐ _____ Lemons
- ☐ _____ Limes
- ☐ _____ Melons
- ☐ _____ Oranges
- ☐ _____ Pears
- ☐ _____ _____
- ☐ _____ _____
- ☐ _____ _____
- ☐ _____ _____

MEAT, FISH, POULTRY

- ☐ _____ Lean beef
- ☐ _____ Lean ground beef
- ☐ _____ Chicken
- ☐ _____ Deli meat
- ☐ _____ Fish
- ☐ _____ Lean ham
- ☐ _____ Low-fat hot dogs
- ☐ _____ Low-fat sausage

- ☐ _____ Pork tenderloin
- ☐ _____ Shellfish
- ☐ _____ Turkey
- ☐ _____ Turkey bacon
- ☐ _____ _____
- ☐ _____ _____
- ☐ _____ _____
- ☐ _____ _____

VEGETABLES

- ☐ _____ Broccoli
- ☐ _____ Cabbage
- ☐ _____ Carrots
- ☐ _____ Cauliflower
- ☐ _____ Celery
- ☐ _____ Cucumbers
- ☐ _____ Garlic
- ☐ _____ Lettuce
- ☐ _____ Mushrooms
- ☐ _____ Onions
- ☐ _____ Peppers
- ☐ _____ Potatoes
- ☐ _____ Radishes
- ☐ _____ Spinach
- ☐ _____ Tomatoes
- ☐ _____ _____
- ☐ _____ _____
- ☐ _____ _____
- ☐ _____ _____

MISCELLANEOUS

- ☐ _____
- ☐ _____
- ☐ _____
- ☐ _____
- ☐ _____
- ☐ _____
- ☐ _____
- ☐ _____
- ☐ _____
- ☐ _____
- ☐ _____
- ☐ _____

FIRST PLACE

Fitness and Activity

PHYSICAL ACTIVITY PROGRAM

WHY SHOULD I BECOME MORE PHYSICALLY ACTIVE?

The Bible says little specifically about physical activity or exercise. First Timothy 4:7,8 speaks only indirectly about the value of bodily exercise.

People who are most successful at starting and sticking with a regular physical activity program generally have strong and enduring motivations for doing so. In other words, physical activity provides them with important and meaningful benefits.

First Timothy 4:7,8 speaks to the benefits of living a lifestyle that is pleasing to God. Taking good care of yourself physically is one way to honor God with your body (see 1 Corinthians 6:19). A healthy and physically fit body will give you the energy and enthusiasm you need to carry out the purposes that God has for your life. Practicing healthy living and self-control are ways to glorify God and become more effective in daily living.

THE BENEFITS OF PHYSICAL ACTIVITY

More than 50 years of scientific and medical evidence indicate that a physically active lifestyle provides many important health and fitness benefits.

Health Benefits

- Lowers risk for heart disease
- Reduces risk for certain cancers
- Lowers blood pressure
- Improves cholesterol levels
- Prevents obesity
- Prevents diabetes

- Builds healthy bones
- Enhances immune function

Fitness Benefits

- Increases aerobic capacity
- Increases strength
- Increases flexibility
- Improves balance and coordination
- Increases functional health

Physical fitness allows you to do the things you want to do and need to do with ease and enjoyment throughout your lifetime.

HOW MUCH PHYSICAL ACTIVITY DO I NEED?

The latest recommendations from experts such as the American Heart Association, the American College of Sports Medicine and the Surgeon General of the United States suggest that you should get 30 minutes or more of moderate-intensity physical activity on most—preferably *all*—days of the week. If you already meet these minimum guidelines, you may receive additional health and fitness benefits from becoming more physically active or including more vigorous activity in your program. The activities you choose should be appropriate for your abilities, needs and interests.

You may notice that the experts no longer use the word "exercise." That's right! You don't have to exercise to get many of the health benefits associated with physical activity.

WHAT DO THESE RECOMMENDATIONS MEAN FOR ME?

These new recommendations are very appropriate in light of Paul's words in 1 Timothy 4:8: "for physical training is of some value." The body is not designed for exercise; it's designed to be physically active. Unfortunately, we live in an environment that has engineered a lot of physical activity out of our lifestyles. Recent reports indicate that up to 60 percent of Americans don't get enough physical activity to improve their health. Because of these facts, a more structured, physically active program often becomes necessary to fit in the activity you need.

The good news is that high levels of exercise are not necessary for good health—regular physical activity is! The key to good health and an appropriate level of fitness is to fit physical activity into your life at a level that is right for you. The only requirements are that the activity be moderate in intensity and add up to at least 30 minutes each day. Increased activity and more vigorous activity may provide additional benefits, but they're only necessary when these benefits are important to you.

How Do I Get Started?

Did you know that 50 percent of people who start an exercise program drop out within the first three to six months? Eventually more than 75 percent of people drop out! You may think that the most important questions to ask when starting a physical activity program are:

- What type of exercise is best?
- How much exercise should I do?
- How hard should I exercise?

To help you make physical activity a part of your lifestyle, the First Place program focuses on a different set of questions. We believe it's more important for you to answer the following questions than it is to start a program that's not right for you.

- What are my goals and motivations?
- What activities do I enjoy?
- How can I fit physical activity into my schedule?
- Who can help me get started and stick with it?
- Do I prefer to exercise alone or with others?
- Do I need routine or variety?
- What has worked for me in the past? What hasn't worked?
- What are my barriers to being active? What are my excuses?

Use the following recommendations and information to help you answer these questions and build your physical activity program.

The First Place Physical Activity Recommendations

We recommend that you set a long-term goal of incorporating the four First Place physical activity recommendations into your lifestyle. The idea is not to start with all four at once. Choose the recommendations and the level of activity that are right for you. Increase the frequency, duration and number of days, adding in the other recommendations (i.e., strength training) as you become ready. Most importantly, set realistic goals and start slowly.

1. **Do *aerobic activity* three to five days each week.**
   Work up to at least 30 minutes of moderate-intensity physical activity (lifestyle activity) on as many days of the week as possible (preferably every day).

   —or—

   Get at least 20 minutes of moderate- to vigorous-intensity physical activity (aerobic exercise) three to five days each week.

   As you become more active and fit, try to do both daily lifestyle activity and regular aerobic exercise.

2. Do *flexibility* (stretching) exercises at least three days each week—preferably every day.

3. Do *strength-training* exercises two to three days each week.

4. Enjoy your health and fitness by participating in enjoyable leisure and recreational activities several times each week.

   Cut down on sedentary activities that cause you to sit for 30 minutes or more at a time (television, desk work, driving, etc.).

UNDERSTANDING THE RECOMMENDATIONS

For most people, becoming more physically active means taking extra steps to fit enjoyable activities into their day. You don't have to do vigorous exercise such as brisk walking, jogging, aerobic dance, bicycling or swimming for at least 30 minutes at a time and at a specific heart rate. Fortunately, many other physical activities, when performed daily, also provide long-term health and fitness benefits. The most important thing is that you choose activities you enjoy.

Use the First Place physical activity recommendations to fit physical activity into your lifestyle at the level that's best for you. If you're currently inactive, start with the lifestyle activities. The latest research reveals that doing 30 minutes of moderate-intensity physical activity—e.g., walking, gardening and yard work, taking the stairs, dancing—every day gives the same benefits as 20 minutes of aerobic exercise—e.g., brisk walking, jogging, aerobic dance, swimming—three days per week. Begin with your favorite aerobic exercise, but start slowly. You can even do a combination of both lifestyle activity and aerobic exercise for greater variety and benefit.

You don't have to break into a sweat, feel your muscles burn or even monitor your heart rate to get the health benefits of physical activity. With moderate activity, you should feel like you are pushing yourself somewhat or working with a purpose. Your pace should cause some increase in breathing but not so much that you can't carry on a conversation. If you can't keep your pace for at least 30 minutes, you're working too hard. You should also feel back to normal within 30 minutes of working out.

Always begin moderate to vigorous activities with a warm-up. A warm-up consists of 5 to 10 minutes of light activity and stretching. A warm-up gradually increases the heart rate and breathing and loosens the muscles and joints for activity. This makes your activity more enjoyable and lowers your risk of injury.

Always end moderate to vigorous activities with a cooldown. A cooldown consists of 5 to 10 minutes of light activity and stretching. A cooldown gradually slows down the heart rate and breathing and helps keep the muscles and joints loose following activity. This may be the best time to do flexibility activities because the muscles and joints are warm and loose.

PLAY IT SAFE!

Moderate-intensity physical activity is safe for most people. In fact, it's associated with several important health benefits, including lowering the risk of heart attack. However, when starting a new physical-activity program, it's best to discuss your plans with your personal physician, particularly if you haven't had a recent health checkup. If you have heart disease, high blood pressure, diabetes, arthritis, osteoporosis, other medical conditions or if you are pregnant, talk to your doctor before starting any activity program. If you're a man over 40 or a woman over 50 and you plan to do vigorous activity, you also need to talk with your doctor before beginning.

Your goal should be to make activity a lifetime habit. Start slowly and progress gradually.

THE ACTIVITY PYRAMID

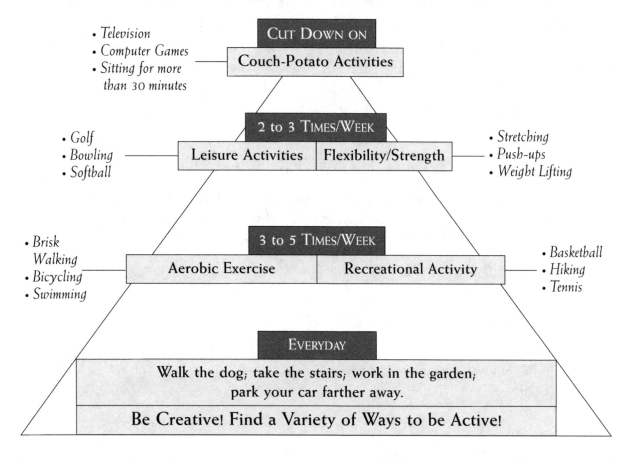

- *Television*
- *Computer Games*
- *Sitting for more than 30 minutes*

CUT DOWN ON

Couch-Potato Activities

2 to 3 TIMES/WEEK

| Leisure Activities | Flexibility/Strength |

- *Golf*
- *Bowling*
- *Softball*

- *Stretching*
- *Push-ups*
- *Weight Lifting*

3 to 5 TIMES/WEEK

| Aerobic Exercise | Recreational Activity |

- *Brisk Walking*
- *Bicycling*
- *Swimming*

- *Basketball*
- *Hiking*
- *Tennis*

EVERYDAY

Walk the dog; take the stairs; work in the garden; park your car farther away.

Be Creative! Find a Variety of Ways to be Active!

THE ACTIVITY PYRAMID—A NEW EXERCISE PRESCRIPTION

For years, experts in health and fitness have been telling us that in order to get the benefits of exercise, we must follow the FITT Prescription.

F —Frequency of at least three to five days each week

I —Intensity of 60 to 90 percent of the maximum heart rate

T —Time of 20 to 60 minutes

T —Type of activities include jogging, aerobic dance, bicycling and swimming

The focus has also been on structured aerobic exercise because it increases fitness and lowers the risk for heart disease, diabetes, high blood pressure, abnormal cholesterol levels and obesity. Unfortunately, less than 25 percent of adults participate in regular exercise at this level.

Fortunately, for the 60 percent of Americans who are not regularly active, new scientific evidence indicates that the FITT Prescription isn't the only way to get the benefits of a physically active lifestyle. A variety of daily activities provide the foundation for good health. The activity pyramid, based on the recommendations of major health and fitness organizations, illustrates a balanced and healthy plan for daily physical activity. It's a simple guide for visualizing how physical activity can fit into your life. With this plan, you choose what works best for you based on your goals, interests and abilities.

PUTTING THE PYRAMID TO WORK FOR YOU

Use the activity pyramid to help you visualize where you are in your physical-activity commitment. If you haven't started yet, use the pyramid to help you get moving. If you're already active, use the pyramid to help you move to the next level.

1. Are you regularly active?

2. Are you participating in a variety of activities?

3. What other enjoyable activities can you add to your program to help you reach your goals?

DAILY LIFESTYLE ACTIVITY

The base of the pyramid includes lifestyle activities that can easily fit into your daily routine. The good news is that lifestyle activities don't have to be done all at one time. Even shorter periods of activity will result in health benefits as long as the total adds up to 30 minutes or more each day. Lifestyle activities such as walking, climbing the stairs, doing housework, playing with the kids and leisure bicycling are great ways to get started on a program of healthy physical activity.

1. What lifestyle activities are you ready to add into your day?

2. If you're not ready to commit to 30 minutes of daily activity, what are the reasons?

3. What can you do to overcome these barriers?

4. Are you willing to ask for the help you need to get started?

5. Do you feel it's important to commit to maintaining a level of physical activity that will result in significant health benefits?

AEROBIC ACTIVITIES

The next level of the pyramid includes aerobic activities. This level follows the more traditional FITT Prescription. Because aerobic activities are typically more vigorous, 20 minutes at least three days each week will provide similar benefits as the daily lifestyle activities. As the variety, intensity and duration of activity increases, the health and fitness benefits increase. The more active you are, the more calories you burn.

1. Are you regularly participating in aerobic activity?

2. What aerobic activities do you enjoy?

3. Are you ready to add these activities into your week?

4. Who can help you get started?

STRENGTH AND FLEXIBILITY

The third level emphasizes strength and flexibility exercises. Flexibility is the ability to move the joints through a full range of motion. It reduces pain and stiffness, prevents injuries and makes you feel better. Flexibility exercises should be performed a minimum of two to three days each week, preferably every day. Muscular strength and endurance are also important for overall health and quality of life. Strong muscles allow you to participate in a variety of daily activities with ease and enjoyment. Strength-building activities should be performed two to three days each week. Performing one set of several different exercises that use all the major muscle groups is all you need. You can use your own body weight, elastic bands or small hand weights.

ONE STEP AT A TIME

Design your program based on your own personal goals and interests. Start with enjoyable activities that fit easily into your lifestyle. Start slowly and make regular activity a habit. Be active every day if you can. If you're having trouble getting started, look for ways to cut down on the time you spend in sedentary activities. Challenge yourself to get up and move even if it's just for a few minutes.

Once physical activity becomes an enjoyable habit, look for new opportunities to fit activity into your day. Add in flexibility and strength exercises when you're ready. You can enjoy your health and fitness by taking time for activities such as hiking, skiing, golf, a local fun run and other recreational activities. Perhaps you can set a long-term goal of doing physical activities from each level of the pyramid every week. Doing a variety of activities from each level is an enjoyable way to achieve total body conditioning.

HOW PHYSICALLY ACTIVE ARE YOU?

Being overweight and obese are increasing at alarming rates in this country. Many experts believe it's not the calories we eat that's causing the problem—it's the calories we don't use! Think back to when you were a child. Did you or your parents: Walk or ride a bike? Use a computer? Do housework with electronic appliances? Mow grass with a self-propelled mower? Have a remote control? Get food from a drive-thru? It's easy to see that our daily lives involve much less physical activity than ever before.

COUNT THE COST

For every hour of moderate physical activity that modern conveniences replace, you lose 200 to 300 calories. Actually, experts estimate that Americans use 500 fewer calories per day than they did 100 years ago. Using computer e-mail 16 minutes a day instead of hand delivering messages will result in a yearly weight gain of 5 to 10 pounds. Notice that Genesis 3:19 doesn't say: "By the turn of a key, the push of a gas pedal and the flip of a switch, you'll get your food from a drive-thru!"

ARE YOU A COUCH POTATO?

We all need to sit and to sleep every day. However, are you sitting more than you should? Select three typical days and keep track of how many hours you spend sleeping and sitting. Use the following chart to record your results. It may be easiest to fill in the chart several times each day, such as after lunch and dinner and before you go to bed. Add up the totals at the end of the day. Most people are surprised by how sedentary they are.

	Day 1	Day 2	Day 3
Sleeping			
Sitting at home			
Sitting at work			
Traveling			
Other			
Total hours			
Average number of hours I spend sleeping and sitting:			

Other Sedentary Activities	
Napping	Desk work
Watching TV	Lying down
Reading	Meeting
Writing	Eating
On the phone	Sewing
Computer	Playing cards

HOW MUCH TIME DO YOU SPEND ON THE MOVE?

Surveys reveal that 25 percent of Americans spend little or no time doing moderate to vigorous physical activity. Yet as little as 30 minutes of moderate physical activity every day results in many important health benefits. Using the following chart, keep track of the number of minutes you spend in moderate to vigorous physical activity for three days. Fill in the chart several times each day. (See the examples in the next section.)

	Day 1	Day 2	Day 3
Moderate			
Vigorous			
Very vigorous			
Total minutes			
Average number of hours I spend doing beneficial physical activity:			

WHAT ARE MODERATE AND VIGOROUS ACTIVITIES?

Moderate-intensity activities are equivalent to walking a mile in 15 to 20 minutes. For most people, moderate-intensity activities will cause some increase in breathing and require some effort, but they will not be uncomfortable. Routine short walks (i.e., to and from your car) only count if you pick up the pace.

Vigorous activities are equivalent to walking uphill. There's a very noticeable increase in breathing and effort. Any activity that seems more difficult than a brisk walk but not as difficult as jogging is a vigorous activity. Very vigorous activities are equivalent to jogging at any speed. These activities are strenuous and increase breathing enough that it's difficult to carry on a conversation.

Even though you may feel you're on your feet and moving around all day, most of your activity is probably light. Light activities include leisurely walking, bowling, playing an instrument, standing, ironing, cooking and general auto repair. You don't need to keep track of your light activities.

Try to estimate as accurately as you can the time you spend moving. For example, some activities only involve short bursts of moderate to hard activity. Also, the intensity of some activities depends on how hard you work. For example, tennis can be light or very hard, depending on how much and how fast you move. Classify the intensity by how it makes you feel.

Moderate Activities	Vigorous Activities	Very Vigorous Activities
Walking (15-20 minutes per mile)	Brisk walking (12-15 minutes per mile)	Jogging
Easy swimming	Swimming laps	Sports such as soccer and basketball
Leisurely biking (5-10 mph)	Climbing stairs (normal pace)	Bicycling (uphill or racing)
Heavy cleaning (car, windows)	Singles tennis	Carrying heavy loads
Carrying light loads	Aerobic Dance	Chopping wood
Mowing with a propelled mower	Mowing with a push mower	Shoveling snow or digging ditches

ADD UP THE TOTALS

To determine the amount of time you spend in light activities, add your sleeping and sitting time to your physical activity time and subtract the result from 24 hours. If any hours are left over, this is the amount of time you spend doing light activities. Many people are surprised to find that nearly 23 hours of their day are spent sleeping, sitting or doing light activities.

MAKE ACTIVITY COUNT

Now that you know where you stand (or sit!), you can begin looking for creative and enjoyable ways to add moderate—maybe even vigorous—physical activities into your daily routine. Replacing just one hour of sedentary activity with moderate activity burns an extra 200 calories or more. Thinking about your typical day, when can you add in extra activity? Be creative and think of as many ideas as you can. Here are some ideas to help fit more activity into your day:

- Look for opportunities to use the stairs instead of the elevator or escalator.
- Do you live in a two-story house? Always use the bathroom on the other floor.
- If you take the elevator at work or while shopping, get off one or two floors early and take the stairs.
- Always park your car farther away at work and when shopping or eating out.
- If you take the bus or taxi, always get off one or two blocks early and walk the rest of the way.
- When watching television or doing desk work, take a physical activity break every 30 minutes. Five to 10 minutes of extra activity several times a day adds up to extra calories burned and improved health!
- When working around the house, pick up the pace—put a little more *umph* in your cleaning!
- Mow your own grass or trade your self-propelled mower for a push model.

TESTING YOUR HEALTH-RELATED FITNESS

Assessing your health-related fitness levels gives you a road map of where you are and where you need to be. However, remember that what you do is more important than how you score on a test. It's important that you're moving toward a level of fitness that allows you to be healthy and accomplish your goals in life. A healthy lifestyle will provide the benefits you need for good health and effective living.

Testing your health-related fitness helps you:

- Develop and maintain an activity program that's right for you.
- Decide where you need the most work.
- Monitor your progress.
- Get back on track if you notice yourself slipping in a few areas.

THE COMPONENTS OF HEALTH-RELATED FITNESS

When assessing your fitness, four components play an important role in your overall health and fitness. A balanced fitness plan will consider each of these areas:

- Cardiovascular endurance (aerobic fitness)
- Muscular strength and endurance
- Flexibility
- Body composition

The health-related fitness standards for each of these assessments serve as guidelines. Use the standards to get a basic understanding of your health-related fitness. Regardless of your scores, you can use these assessments to help you monitor your progress. If you fall below the standards listed for one or more of the fitness components, you may need to do some work in those areas. What's most important is that you're participating in a variety of enjoyable and beneficial physical activities.

THE HEALTH-RELATED FITNESS TESTS

A Note on Safety

While these tests should not pose any special risk for most people, it's important to take a few precautions. If you have any underlying medical problems, such as heart disease or arthritis, talk to your doctor before taking any of these assessments. Don't push yourself to your limits on any of these tests. The idea is to learn what you can do comfortably and then use the results to monitor your progress.

- Wear comfortable clothing and shoes appropriate for brisk walking. Avoid taking the tests on days when it's extremely hot, cold or windy.

- Have a friend or family member help you with the tests.

- Before performing any tests, warm-up for five minutes with light activity and stretching. Cool down when you have finished.

- If you experience any pain or discomfort during any part of the assessments, stop immediately and consult your physician.

1. *How Physically Active Are You?*

It's much more important to keep track of your physical activity than it is to know your fitness level. As you increase your physical activity, your health and fitness will improve. Regular aerobic activity is associated with several important benefits, such as a lowered risk for heart disease, improved mood and maintenance of a healthy weight.

I exercise at least three days each week for 30 minutes at a time doing vigorous activities such as walking briskly, jogging, bicycling, aerobic dance or aerobic sports such as soccer, tennis or basketball.	True	False
I am physically active for at least 30 minutes on most days of the week doing moderate intensity activities throughout the day such as brisk walking, yard work, leisurely bicycling, swimming, taking the stairs, playing with the kids or other activities.	True	False

Recommendations: Hopefully your goal is to work up to meeting one or both of these physical activity standards. These standards represent the level of physical activity necessary for good health. If you're not yet meeting at least one of these standards, plan to get started as soon as you can. However, start slow and gradually work your way up. Start with 5 or 10 minutes doing an activity that you enjoy. If you're meeting the above standards, you're already doing more than most people. Keep up the good work! Working up to three to five hours of moderate to vigorous activity each week will give you additional fitness benefits and help you achieve and maintain a healthy weight.

2. *How Aerobically Fit Are You?*

Cardiovascular endurance is important to overall health and fitness. There are a number of ways to assess your cardiovascular endurance and monitor your progress. One of the easiest and safest ways is to do a one-mile walk test.

What You Will Need

- A flat surface that allows you to measure off a one-mile distance, such as a track at a local school, a walking path at a park, a shopping mall, etc.
- A stopwatch or a watch with a seconds indicator to keep track of your time.

What to Do

Practice taking your pulse several times before the taking the assessment. Then walk a mile as quickly as you can without straining. At the end of the mile, record your time in minutes and seconds. You may also want to take your pulse for 15 seconds immediately upon stopping. Multiply your pulse by 4 to get the number of heartbeats per minute.

Health-Related Fitness Standard

A good time is between 15 and 20 minutes (closer to 15 minutes if you're younger than 50). If you can walk the mile in less than 14 minutes, you're doing great.

Recommendations: If you can walk one mile in at least 15 to 20 minutes and you're meeting the activity standard, keep up the good work. To monitor your progress, repeat the test every 6 to 12 weeks. As your fitness improves you'll be able to cover the distance in less time, and if you're monitoring your heart rate, you may also notice a gradual drop. If you meet the aerobic fitness standard but not the activity standard, don't get too confident. The only way to maintain your fitness level and get the health benefits you need is to be active regularly.

---

3. *How Fit Are Your Muscles?*

Muscular strength and endurance are important aspects of health and fitness, particularly as we age. As you lose strength, daily activities become more difficult. Healthy muscles allow you to participate in a variety of activities with ease and enjoyment. Unfortunately, muscular fitness declines as we age. The only way to maintain healthy muscles is to exercise them on a regular basis. Take the following two tests to assess your muscular strength and endurance.

CURL-UPS

This assessment tests the strength and endurance of the abdominal (stomach) muscles. Weak stomach muscles contribute to lower-back pain that affects millions of adults. The best way to strengthen your stomach muscles is to do curl-ups.

What You Will Need
- A carpeted surface or an exercise mat
- A partner to hold your legs and count your curl-ups
- A stopwatch or a watch with a seconds indicator to keep track of your time

What to Do
- Lie on your back with your feet flat on the floor and knees bent at a 90-degree angle.
- Fold your arms across your chest.
- Curl up slowly by lifting your shoulders off the ground. Continue to raise your body until your elbows touch your knees. Don't lift up to a sitting position.
- Exhale during the upward movement and inhale on the way down. Don't hold your breath!
- Do as many curl-ups as you comfortably can without straining. Stop at one minute.

Health-Related Fitness Standard
If you can do 15 to 20 curl-ups, you're doing well. If you can do 30 or more, you're doing great.

PUSH-UPS

Doing push-ups is a good way to assess the strength and endurance of your upper body.

What You Will Need
- A carpeted surface or an exercise mat
- A partner to count your push-ups and watch your form
- A stopwatch or a watch with a seconds indicator to keep track of your time

What to Do
- Lie face down with hands a shoulder width apart, palms face down and legs extended straight back. Women should cross their ankles and push up with their knees on the ground.
- Keeping your back and legs straight, push yourself up with your arms, shoulders and chest until your arms are straight.
- Lower yourself back down until your chest touches the floor.
- Exhale during the upward movement and inhale on the way down. Don't hold your breath!
- Do as many push-ups as you comfortably can without straining. Stop at one minute.

Health-Related Fitness Standard:
If you can do 10 to 15 push-ups, you're doing well. If you can do 25 or more, you're doing great.

Recommendations: Experts recommend doing at least two days of strength training each week. It's best to do at least one set of 8 to 10 exercises that work each of the major muscle groups—shoulders, back, chest, arms and legs. You can do strength-building exercises using your own body weight, elastic exercise bands, hand and ankle weights, dumbbells or machines. Are you doing strength-building activities regularly?

4. How Flexible Are You?

It's important to maintain flexibility. Poor flexibility increases feelings of stiffness, limits mobility and may increase the risk of certain injuries. Take the following test to assess your flexibility.

SIT AND REACH

This assessment tests the flexibility of the backs of your legs (the hamstring muscles), hips and lower back.

What You Will Need
- A carpeted surface or an exercise mat
- A yardstick and a strip of masking tape
- A partner to measure your stretch and watch your form

What to Do
- Place the yardstick on the floor and put a long strip of masking tape across the yardstick at the 15-inch mark.
- Sit on the floor with your legs extended, straddling the yardstick. Your feet should be 10 to 12 inches apart. Place your heels at the 15-inch mark with the 0 mark close to you.
- With one hand on top of the other and fingertips even, slowly lean forward as far as you comfortably can along the yardstick. Exhale as you stretch forward and be sure not to bend your knees. Don't bounce or overstretch.
- Perform the test three times and take your best measurement to the nearest inch.

Health-Related Fitness Standard
A good score is 12 to 18 inches. There's probably no health advantage to being able to stretch beyond these limits.

Recommendations: To increase or maintain your flexibility, perform several stretching activities at least three days each week; do them every day if you can. Never stretch to the point of pain, and avoid bouncing or jerking movements. Hold each stretch for 10 to 20 seconds. Avoid stretches that put pressure on your neck, lower back or knees.

---

5. How's Your Body Composition?

Body composition refers to the portion of your weight that is made up of fat or muscle. A lean and muscular body is healthier than a body with too much fat. The best tests for body composition are underwater weighing or skin-fold measurements. You can also use your body-mass index and waist measurement to determine your health-related body composition.

BODY-MASS INDEX (BMI)	WAIST SIZE
In most people, BMI provides an accurate reflection of body composition and health risk. Here's how you calculate your BMI: • Multiply your current weight in pounds by 703. • Divide the result by your height in inches. • Divide the result by your height in inches again. **Health-Related Fitness Standard** A body-mass index between 21 to 25 is the healthiest range. A BMI above 30 is classified as obesity and is associated with a high health risk.	Your waist size is also a good measure of the amount of fat you carry in your abdomen. To measure your waist, measure around the smallest part of your waistline in inches. Don't pull in, just stand relaxed. The narrowest part of your waistline is usually at the level of your hipbone and near your belly button. **Health-Related Standard** A waist measurement greater than 35 inches for women and 40 inches for men indicates a much higher risk of weight-related health problems.

Recommendations: Monitor your BMI and waist measurement periodically to monitor your progress. Because the scale doesn't always reflect what's happening to your body weight, it's best to pay attention to your waistline and how you feel. Are your clothes fitting differently? Is your waistline getting smaller? These are often better indicators of healthy weight loss than following the numbers on the scale. Your lifestyle is more important than your weight, BMI or waistline. Focus on healthy eating and regular physical activity.

STARTING A WALKING PROGRAM

Walking may be the ideal exercise. It can be done just about anywhere, any time and with little expense. All it takes is a good pair of shoes and a safe place. No skill is required, and the risk of injury is low. It can fit into your schedule whether you have two minutes or two hours. Walking is powerful medicine. It improves your health, lowers your risk of disease and adds quality to your life.

THE BENEFITS OF WALKING

- Helps prevent and control heart disease, stroke and diabetes
- Helps you reach and maintain a desirable body weight
- Lowers your risk of several types of cancer
- Increases the strength of your heart, lungs, muscles and bones
- Reduces high blood pressure
- Improves blood cholesterol levels
- Promotes psychological well being

HOW DO I GET STARTED?

By working up to just 30 minutes of walking three or more days each week, you can reap the benefits of an active lifestyle. Here's a checklist to help get you started.
- Make room in your schedule for a regular walk.
- Ask for help from family or friends to get started and stick with your walking program.
- Choose two or three safe and convenient places to walk (track, trail, treadmill, mall or sidewalk).
- Make sure you have comfortable clothing, well-cushioned shoes and a water bottle.
- Find a walking partner or use headphones with music to help you stay motivated.
  Be careful: Don't let headphones distract you from traffic and other hazards!

WALKING: BENEFITS AT ANY AGE

Studies reported in major medical journals confirm that walking can provide important health benefits for men and women of all ages. One study reported in the *New England Journal of Medicine* found that retired men walking at least two miles each day lowered their risk of dying early from all causes by 50 percent compared to men who walked little. Walking has proven equally beneficial for women.

How fast do I have to walk to get these benefits? The great news is that you don't have to huff and puff to get these important health benefits. The idea is to walk at a pace that pushes you—gets your heart beating faster, warms your muscles and causes you to breathe a little harder. Pick the pace that's right for you. If you can walk a mile in 15 to 20 minutes, you're doing great.

Is more walking better? People successful in long-term weight loss have reported walking 45 to 60 minutes a day. However, the idea is not to walk more but to walk regularly. Make walking a lifetime commitment. Don't get burned out by doing too much too soon. Thirty minutes of brisk walking at least three days a week will give you most of the health benefits you need. If you don't have 30 minutes at one time, three 10-minute walks are just as beneficial.

RUNNING YOUR WAY TO HEALTH AND FITNESS

Running is an excellent form of aerobic exercise. It can be done almost anywhere and any time. It takes little skill and little special equipment. Running burns a high number of calories in a short amount of time. It can be done alone, with a partner or in a group. However, running isn't for everyone, and it's not necessary for health and fitness. There are a lot of great ways to exercise and be physically active; the most important thing is that you choose what you enjoy.

STARTING OFF ON THE RIGHT FOOT

Talk with your doctor before starting a running program. To run enjoyably and safely requires a moderate to high level of fitness. If you've been inactive for a while, have joint problems or are overweight, it's best to start with a walking program or another moderate activity and then progress to running as your fitness improves. Despite popular belief, running doesn't cause joint problems in most people.

EQUIPMENT

The great thing about running is that it requires little equipment. The most important equipment is a good pair of shoes. Running in improper or worn-out shoes can cause injuries; however, the majority of injuries associated with running are caused by doing too much too soon.

Running shoes should be lightweight and have extra cushioning in the heel and forefoot for shock absorption. Good arch support is important too. The heel should fit snugly. Make sure you have plenty of toe room—about a thumb's width between the end of the shoe and your toes is recommended. Every foot is different, so you have to find the shoe that's right for you. Try on several pairs before buying—jog in the store to find the pair that fits best.

If you're running in warm or hot weather, your clothes should be lightweight and loose fitting. Light-colored clothing is usually best. Cotton is a good choice, but newer fabrics that pull moisture away from your body are best. Sunglasses, a cap and sunscreen are important.

When it's cold outside, it's better to wear several lightweight layers rather than one heavy layer. The inner layer should be a fabric that pulls moisture away from your body. Choose an outer layer that blocks the wind and moisture. As your body warms up, you can remove a layer of clothing. A hat and gloves may be your best defense against the cold.

LOCATION

You can run anywhere—in your neighborhood, at the park, on a track or on a treadmill at home or a fitness club. Wherever you choose to run, be sure it's convenient, enjoyable and safe. Consider the following when choosing a location:

- Choose a safe place to run, with little traffic and few obstacles. Always try to run against traffic so you can see approaching vehicles.

- Use good judgment when running at night. Run on well-lit streets, and consider taking a partner with you. Always let someone know where you are going and when you will return. Make sure you wear light-colored and reflective clothing.

- A track can be a great place to run. It has a special surface, you're never too far from where you started and you can easily measure your distance. On a regular-sized track, four laps will equal a mile. It's best to run on smooth and flat surfaces to lower your risk of injury.

GETTING STARTED—A SAMPLE PROGRAM

Start with walking. Make sure you can walk briskly for at least 20 to 30 minutes several days a week before moving on to a running program. Once you're comfortable with walking and your fitness improves, you can begin by running short distances during your walk. Try to work out at least three days during each week of the program. If you find a particular week's pattern tiring, repeat it before going on to the next level. Progress according to your goals and how you feel. You don't have to complete the program in 12 weeks.

	Warm-Up (Walk slowly)	Walk/Run Program (Walk briskly/ run slowly)	Cooldown (Walk slowly)	Total Time
Week 1	5 minutes	5 minutes/1 minute	5 minutes	20 to 30 minutes
Week 2	5 minutes	4 minutes /1 minute	5 minutes	20 to 30 minutes
Week 3	5 minutes	5 minutes/2 minutes	5 minutes	20 to 30 minutes
Week 4	5 minutes	4 minutes/2 minutes	5 minutes	20 to 30 minutes
Week 5	5 minutes	5 minutes/3 minutes	5 minutes	20 to 30 minutes
Week 6	5 minutes	4 minutes/3 minutes	5 minutes	20 to 30 minutes
Week 7	5 minutes	5 minutes/5 minutes	5 minutes	20 to 30 minutes
Week 8	5 minutes	5 minutes/8 minutes	5 minutes	20 to 30 minutes
Week 9	5 minutes	10 minutes/10 minutes	5 minutes	30 minutes
Week 10	5 minutes	5 minutes/15 minutes	5 minutes	30 minutes
Week 11	5 minutes	20 minutes	5 minutes	30 minutes

Week 12
Once you get to 20 minutes of running three days per week, consider your options:

- Stay where you are. Twenty minutes of running three days per week will give you the aerobic benefits that you need for good health.

- Add another day of walking or jogging. Start at week 1 and follow the schedule for increasing your time on that day.

- Begin running faster, increasing your pace gradually over a period of several weeks. One way to increase your pace is to run faster for one to three minutes; then slow down for three to five minutes or until your breathing has returned to normal. This is called interval training. Start with one interval each workout; then add an interval each week or when you're ready.

- Increase your running time by three to five minutes each week or as you feel ready.

- Add a new activity to your fitness program such as swimming, aerobic dance, bicycling or strength training. Remember to start slowly and work your way up gradually.

Tips

- Run at a pace that feels comfortable. If running leaves you so short of breath that you can't keep up a conversation, it's too intense.

- Stay relaxed when you run. Keep your back straight, shoulders back and head up. Swing your arms freely at about the level of your hips and keep your hands relaxed. Breathe out of your nose or mouth naturally. Land on your heel, keep your toes pointed forward, roll your foot forward and push off with the ball of your foot. Maintain a smooth stride and avoid bouncing.

- Learn some basic stretches for the lower back, legs, calves and ankles. Do these before and after you run.

- Drink plenty of water before, during and after your run. Don't wait until you feel thirsty to drink.

- If anything hurts, take time off until it feels better. Perhaps you did too much too soon.

- Check your shoes. Are they in good condition? Do they have enough padding and support? Replace your shoes when they become worn.

- Keep a training diary to monitor your progress.

- Thousands of people train for local fun runs or competitions each year. Completing a run can give you a great sense of accomplishment. Find a run in your area and start training!

BICYCLING YOUR WAY TO HEALTH AND FITNESS

Bicycling is terrific exercise. It provides a great aerobic workout and strengthens the muscles of the lower body, such as the thighs, hips and buttocks. One of the best things about bicycling is that it's low impact—it's easy on the bones and joints. The upper body and arms also get a workout when climbing hills or riding a stationary bike with arm levers. Cycling outdoors can give you a wonderful sense of exhilaration and excitement.

Stationary bicycles are inexpensive and can fit in almost any room in the house. Stationary cycles leave you no excuses for not working out when the weather is bad or your time is limited.

WHICH BIKE IS BEST FOR ME?

Ask yourself what type of riding you'll be doing.
- Do you want to ride indoors or outdoors?
- Will you be riding in the neighborhood, on a bike trail (paved or dirt) or on country roads?
- Do you plan to ride long distances—greater than 20 miles?
- How much money do you want to spend? Bicycles can range from $150 to over $2,000.
- Once you purchase your bike, check it each time before you ride to ensure it's in good repair.

Outdoor Bicycles

- Racing bicycles are lightweight, have narrow tires and dropped handlebars. Most have 10 to 14 gears.
- Mountain bicycles are very popular because they can be used on or off the road. They have wide tires and upright handlebars, and they provide a softer ride than racing bikes. All these make for a more comfortable ride. They have from 18 to 24 gears.
- Hybrid bicycles are a cross between a racing and a mountain bike.
- Unless you plan to ride short distances on flat roads, buy a bicycle with 10 or more gears.

Stationary Bicycles

- Choose a bike with a smooth pedaling motion.
- Make sure you're comfortable with the pedaling resistance and that it's easily adjusted.
- A comfortable and adjustable (tilt) seat is a must. If bicycle seats are typically uncomfortable for you, look for a recumbent bike that will allow you to sit in a padded chair with your legs extended in front of you.
- Some bikes have arm levers that allow you to work your upper body, too.

The Proper Fit

It's important to buy a bicycle that fits. A specialty shop can help you select a bike that meets your needs.

- ➟ The handlebars should be in a position that allows you to relax your shoulders and arms. You should be able to reach the brake levers easily.
- ➟ The seat height should allow your knees to be only slightly bent when the pedals are in the lowest position. Position your feet so the balls of your feet are in the center of the pedals. If your seat is too high, your hips will rock back and forth when you pedal. A seat that's too low puts extra stress on your knees.
- ➟ The tilt of the saddle should be parallel to the ground. If the seat is tilted downward, you'll have to use your arms to hold your body up. A seat that's tilted too high puts too much pressure on your crotch.

Shoes, Clothing and Gear

While not necessary, special cycling clothing can make your ride more pleasant.

- ➟ Shoes can really make a difference. You can wear a comfortable pair of tennis shoes or choose bicycling shoes. These specialty shoes are lightweight and can improve the efficiency of your pedaling. If you plan to ride longer distances, bicycling shoes are a must. Some pedals and shoes are designed to work together. These take more skill to use because your shoes actually clip directly onto the pedals.
- ➟ Bicycling shorts are a good investment no matter what type of riding you plan to do. You can buy tight or loose-fitting shorts with a special pad that provides cushioning, absorbs moisture and prevents chafing.
- ➟ Bicycling shirts are good for riding outdoors because they're tight fitting and cut down on wind resistance. The newer fabrics pull moisture away from your body. Bike shirts also have special pockets for extra gear.
- ➟ Bicycling gloves improve comfort by providing padding for your hands.
- ➟ Sunglasses or protective eyewear for the weather conditions are important. Even if the sun is not shining brightly, the UV rays can be damaging to unprotected eyes.
- ➟ Carry along one or two water bottles. You need to drink water frequently when bicycling. Because of the airflow, you may not realize you're sweating.

Selecting a Helmet

A helmet is your most important piece of equipment. Helmets save lives; never ride without one! The helmet should fit snugly and comfortably. It should have adjustable straps that can be buckled below the jaw. The helmet must be certified by the American National Standards Institute (ANSI) or the Snell Foundation.

Other safety considerations include avoiding riding in high traffic areas or at night and keeping your bike in good repair.

GETTING STARTED—A SAMPLE BICYCLING PROGRAM

Try to ride at least three days during each week of the program. If you find a particular week's pattern tiring, repeat it before going on to the next level. Progress according to your goals and how you feel. You don't have to complete the cycling program in eight weeks. A brisk ride increases your breathing slightly, but not so much that you can't carry on a conversation.

	Warm-Up (Ride slowly)	Walk/Run Program (Ride moderate to vigorous)	Cooldown (Ride slowly)	Total Time
Week 1	5 minutes	10 minutes	5 minutes	20 minutes
Week 2	5 minutes	12 minutes	5 minutes	22 minutes
Week 3	5 minutes	15 minutes	5 minutes	25 minutes
Week 4	5 minutes	17 minutes	5 minutes	27minutes
Week 5	5 minutes	20 minutes	5 minutes	30 minutes
Week 6	5 minutes	25 minutes	5 minutes	35 minutes
Week 7	5 minutes	30 minutes	5 minutes	40 minutes

Week 8

Once you get to 30 minutes of brisk cycling, you may want to consider some new options:

- Add another day. Start at Week One and follow the schedule for the day you're adding.

- Begin riding faster, increasing your pace gradually over a period of several weeks. One way to increase your pace is to ride faster for one to three minutes; then slow down for three to five minutes or until your breathing has returned to normal. This is called interval training. Start with one interval each workout; then add an interval each week or when you're ready.

- Increase the time you spend riding by three to five minutes each week or as you feel ready.

- Add a new activity to your fitness program such as swimming, aerobic dance, walking or strength training. Remember to start slowly and work your way up gradually.

WATER EXERCISE FOR FITNESS AND HEALTH

One great way to add variety and fun to your fitness program is with activities such as water aerobics, water walking and swimming. Water is great for exercise because it provides resistance, keeps you cool, supports your body weight (it's low impact!) and you don't have to worry about traffic. Why water? Check out the benefits:

- Adds fun and enjoyment
- Decreases body fat
- Improves body awareness, balance and coordination
- Increases flexibility
- Increases muscle strength
- Improves aerobic fitness
- Low impact—lowers the chance of injury while exercising
- Improves mood and self-esteem

GETTING STARTED

Walking and jogging are probably the easiest activities you can do in the water. Wearing shoes designed for water walking (water socks) can protect your feet and increase your traction, but they're not necessary. Simply start at one end of the pool and walk back and forth from end to end. To increase the intensity, swing your arms back and forth in the water. The deeper the water the greater the resistance and the more you rely on your balancing skills. You can even buy a flotation vest for deep-water running. Water gloves, water weights and similar equipment can be used to add variety to your workout.

SWIMMING TIPS

Swimming is a great all-around workout both for aerobic fitness and muscle building. And it's easy on the joints. If you're just beginning, start slowly and swim short distances. If you need to rest between laps, keep moving by walking. As you become more fit, you can increase the speed and distance you swim. Your goal is to work up to about 30 minutes of moderate to vigorous movement in the water.

Here are some helpful hints to get you started:

- If you're just starting out, use a modified breaststroke or backstroke that allows you to keep your head out of the water. Use a froglike kick for mobility.
- Once coordination and fitness improve, add a freestyle (front crawl) stroke.
- Goggles, earplugs, caps, snorkels and fins can often make you feel more comfortable in the water.

- If you're not comfortable swimming, take lessons. Many community centers, YMCAs and fitness centers offer lessons as well as fitness swimming sessions.
- Find a partner or two to go with you.

WATER AEROBICS

Many health clubs, YMCAs and community centers offer water-aerobics classes. These classes are designed for all age groups and abilities. Many use the same basic movements you find in regular aerobics classes. In addition to being a beneficial physical activity, this is a great way to enjoy the friendship that comes from working out with a group. If you have a pool at home and want to do an aerobic workout on your own, here are some activities to try:

- Walk or jog in waist- or chest-deep water for several minutes. You can also step and jog in place.
- To improve balance and trunk strength, walk as quickly as you can and then freeze. Repeat this several times.
- Do several minutes of knee lifts using alternating legs—the intensity and speed should be moderate to vigorous. For variety, lift your knees toward the opposite side of your body.
- Do front, back and side kicks using the pool wall or a kickboard.
- Stride back and forth across the pool by taking long (lunging) steps.
- Continue moving by taking long steps sideways along the length of the pool.
- To strengthen the outer and inner thighs, do jumping jacks with your hands in or out of the water.
- Purchase water weights, hand paddles, elastic resistance bands or even a plastic ball to do upper-body strengthening exercises.
- You can even buy an underwater stepping bench for variety. Do front and side steps using the bench.
- After your workout, cool down by slowly walking through the water.
- Keep moving and have fun. Do any combination of activities you like or make up your own.
- Do this three to five days per week or alternate with other aerobic and strengthening activities.
- Add music to liven up your workout.

More Water Activity Tips

- Regardless of which water activities you choose, begin each workout with a 5 to 10-minute warm-up of easy walking and flexibility exercises. You can do these in the water if you want. Take a few minutes to cool down after your workout, too.
- When exercising in water, your heart rate tends to be several beats lower. Pay attention to how you feel rather than trying to reach your target heart rate.
- If outdoors, remember to wear sunscreen and protective clothing. You're not limited to the traditional bathing suit any more. Many companies make special water wear. Avoid getting too hot or cold.
- Even though you're surrounded by water, don't forget to drink. Keep a water bottle with you so that you can drink during your exercise.

Make a Plan of Action

Answer the following questions:

- Do you think that water exercise might be for you?
- Have you tried water exercise before? Did you enjoy it? Is it something you can stick with?
- What steps can you take to get started?
- Do you have access to a convenient indoor or outdoor pool?
- Whom can you call or talk to about getting started with a group class?
- Can you start your own class at a neighborhood pool?
- Check with a local sports or swimming store for special accessories such as shoes, weights, step, kickboard, hand paddles and other gear.

MONITORING YOUR EXERCISE INTENSITY

You may have heard that to get the benefits of aerobic exercise you have to exercise within your heart-rate zone. Perhaps you are monitoring your exercise heart rate already. While it's more important to pay attention to how you feel during an activity, monitoring your heart rate can be a helpful tool. If you want to use your heart rate to monitor your exercise intensity, use the following worksheet to calculate your personal heart rate zone.

HOW SHOULD PHYSICAL ACTIVITY FEEL?

A beneficial level of physical activity will feel like you're pushing yourself somewhat. The activity should cause some increase in breathing, but you should still be able to carry on a conversation. If you can't keep up the intensity for at least 30 minutes, you're working too hard. You should also feel back to normal within 30 minutes after a workout. You don't have to break into a sweat or feel your muscles burn to get the health and fitness benefits of physical activity.

WHY SHOULD I MONITOR MY EXERCISE HEART RATE?

To deliver oxygen to your muscles during activity, your heart must pump stronger and faster. The harder you work, the faster your heart beats. Because your heart rate reflects the intensity of exercise, you can use it to monitor how hard you're working. Researchers have determined that exercising at 60 to 85 percent of your predicted maximum heart rate results in significant health and fitness benefits.

WHAT IS A PREDICTED MAXIMUM HEART RATE?

Everyone has a maximum heart rate. When your heart reaches its limit, the muscles can't get all the oxygen they need, so your body has to slow down. Fortunately, it's not necessary to work at this maximum level to get the benefits of aerobic exercise. Most people don't know their true maximum heart rate; however, you can calculate your predicted maximum heart rate.

Simply subtract your age from 220.

220 – _____ (your age) = _____ maximum heart rate

Once you know your predicted maximum heart rate, you can determine your calculated heart-rate zone. To find your zone, multiply your maximum heart rate by 60 and 85 percent.

Maximum heart rate _____ x .60 = _____ lower end of zone

Maximum heart rate _____ x .85 = _____ higher end of zone

THE FITT PRESCRIPTION

The traditional exercise prescription is based on a *frequency* of at least three days each week, an *intensity* of 60 to 85 percent of maximum heart rate and a *time* of at least 20 minutes of aerobic exercise per session. Studies show that following the FITT prescription (see pp.79-81) significantly increases your aerobic fitness.

Taking Your Resting Heart Rate

Before you can take your exercise heart rate, you need to learn how to find your pulse. The best place to record your pulse is at your wrist. The pulse is found on the outside of your wrist about an inch below the base of your thumb. Turn your palm up and feel for your pulse with the tips of your middle and ring fingers. A light touch is usually all it takes. You can also find the pulse on the side of your neck. Lift your head slightly and use the tips of your fingers to feel to the side of your Adam's apple. Press lightly and move your fingers until you feel your pulse.

Once you're comfortable with finding your pulse, you can move on to counting your resting heart rate. To determine your heart rate use any watch or clock that counts seconds. You'll get the most accurate reading by counting the number of beats for a full 60 seconds. This will give you your heart rate in beats per minute.

Your resting heart rate is a good way to monitor improvements in your fitness. As your body becomes more physically fit, your resting heart rate often falls by several beats. Your heart beats slower because a fit heart pumps more blood with each beat. To keep track of your resting heart rate, take your heart rate before getting out of bed in the morning (make sure you are well rested). Do this periodically to check your progress.

Taking Your Exercise Heart Rate

Once you're comfortable finding your pulse and taking your resting heart rate, you're ready to monitor your heart rate during physical activity. The technique of taking your heart rate during exercise is the same. You'll need to slow down your activity to find your pulse (e.g., gently walk in place). Because your heart rate drops rapidly when you stop exercising, you'll need to find your pulse quickly and count your heart rate for only 15 seconds. To calculate your 15-second heart-rate zone, divide your 60- and 85-percent zones by 4.

Your activity heart-rate zone for a 15-second count:

60% heart rate _____ ÷ 4 = _____

85% heart rate _____ ÷ 4 = _____

These are the two numbers you need to memorize to monitor your exercise intensity. Take your pulse every 5 to 10 minutes during activity to see if you're in your target range. Working at the lower end of the zone should feel moderate to somewhat difficult, and the higher end should feel somewhat difficult to difficult. Because your heart-rate zone is only an estimate, you may need to adjust or personalize your zone. Use the following intensity scale to help you set your personal heart-rate zone.

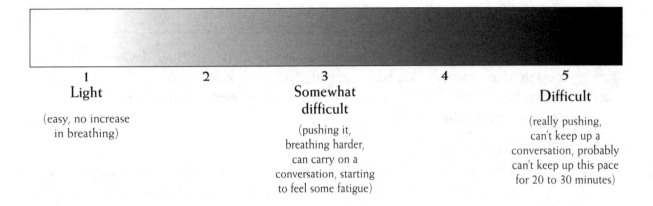

1	2	3	4	5
Light		**Somewhat difficult**		**Difficult**
(easy, no increase in breathing)		(pushing it, breathing harder, can carry on a conversation, starting to feel some fatigue)		(really pushing, can't keep up a conversation, probably can't keep up this pace for 20 to 30 minutes)

Over the next few weeks as you take your heart rate, also try to rate how you feel during your activity. Generally your intensity should fall between a level of 2 and 4. If the activity feels light or difficult, you're probably outside your training range. Most likely your calculated heart-rate zone was accurate, but you may need to adjust it up or down to get a more accurate or personal heart-rate zone.

FITTING IN STRENGTH TRAINING

Strong muscles and bones are important for good health and an active life. While some loss of strength is a part of aging, most people lose strength because they don't get enough physical activity. To ensure that you have the energy, independence and mobility you need for a full and productive life, it's important to include some strength training in your physical activity program.

Studies find that strength training results in several important health benefits. Here's how the health and fitness benefits of strength training compare to aerobic exercise:

Health and Fitness Component	Strength Training	Aerobic Excercise
Increases ability to work and play	+ + +	+ + +
Improves balance in old age	+ + +	+ + +
Lowers blood pressure	+	+ +
Improves blood sugar	+ +	+ + +
Lowers body fat	+ + +	+ + +
Increases bone density	+ + +	+ +
Improves blood cholesterol levels	+	+ +
Increases strength	+ + +	+
Increases metabolic rate	+ +	+ +
Increases muscle mass	+ + +	+ +

+ Some benefit   + + Strong benefit   + + + Very strong benefit

Regular strength training gives you a new awareness of your body, makes you feel more firm and toned, increases metabolism and enhances quality of life by promoting mobility, maintaining strength and reducing risk of chronic disease.

DID YOU KNOW?

Studies show that muscles and bones never lose their responsiveness to strength training; strength gains of nearly 200 percent have been achieved in 80- and 90-year-old men and women.

A study reported in the *Journal of the American Medical Association* found that women over age 50 significantly increased their muscle strength and bone density with regular weight training twice a week. The women in this study increased their strength by 75 percent and their bone density by 1 percent. The women who did no strength training lost strength, muscle mass and bone density.

A study in the elderly found that 12 weeks of resistance training increased daily energy expenditure by 15 percent.

HOW TO BEGIN A STRENGTH-TRAINING PROGRAM

Strength training does not require a lot of equipment or a health-club membership. Strength training can be done at home, in the office or just about anywhere!

Experts recommend that you include strength training in your activity routine two to three times each week. The goal is to find a resistance you can lift between 8 to 15 times without straining. Include at least one exercise for each of the major muscles: shoulders, back, chest, arms, stomach and legs.

CHOOSING EQUIPMENT

You can increase your strength simply by using your own body weight. No equipment is needed! Exercises that don't require special equipment include crunches (a type of sit-up), deep knee bends and push-ups. Add handheld weights, ankle weights or elastic exercise bands, and you have all you need for a complete program at home, at work or on the road.

TIPS FOR GETTING STARTED

- Whether you choose to use weight machines, handheld weights, elastic bands or your own body weight, the method for training remains the same.
- You only need to do strength exercises two or three days each week.
- When first starting, you only need to do each exercise one time or one set.
- Choose a resistance you can do 8 to 15 times without straining too hard or fatiguing the muscle completely. When first starting a strength-training program, it's best to start with very light resistance.
- Don't hold your breath and don't strain. Breathe easily throughout the exercise.
- Do some stretching and light activity before starting to warm up and when finished to cool down.

EXERCISES TO GET YOU STARTED

DEEP KNEE BENDS

Stand in front of a sturdy chair. The seat should be higher than the level of your knees. Keeping your back straight, bend at the knees and hips as if you were going to sit down. As your rear touches the chair's edge, slowly stand back up. If this is too difficult, start by sitting in the chair with your rear scooted toward the front. From this sitting position, stand up. Push off with your hands if you need to. Sit down normally and repeat.

PUSH-UPS

Lie on your stomach, placing your hands shoulder-width apart at chest level. Keeping your back straight and both knees on the floor, push your body away from the floor in one smooth motion. Once your arms are straight, lower yourself back down. As you get stronger, do the push-ups while lifting your knees off the ground too. For an easier version, do the push-up leaning against the wall. Slowly bend at the elbows, allowing your chest to move toward the wall. Push your body away from the wall in one smooth motion.

CRUNCHES

Lie on your back with knees bent at a 90-degree angle. Cross your hands over your chest or rest them on your legs. Slowly lift and curl your upper back and shoulder blades off the floor. You only need to lift your shoulders a few inches off the floor. You should feel some tightness in your stomach. Slowly curl back down.

ARM CURLS

Stand or sit with your arms hanging at your side and palms facing away from your body. Working only one arm at a time, keep your elbows close to your side as you slowly lift a handheld weight or elastic band (stand on the opposite end of the band or tie it to a table leg) by curling the weight up to your shoulder. Lower and repeat. Repeat with the opposite arm.

HOW TO PROGRESS

When 8 to 15 repetitions of any given exercise become easy, you may be ready to progress to the next level. Here are some ideas for the next step:

- Stay where you are.
- Add a few more repetitions.
- Increase the weight or resistance.
- Repeat the exercise twice or even three times as your strength increases.
- Learn new exercises.

A FLEXIBLE FITNESS PROGRAM

Stretching is a simple and relaxing activity that offers a variety of important health and fitness benefits. A regular program of stretching exercises gives you increased flexibility in your muscles and joints which helps you feel more relaxed, prevents injury and improves your ease of movement. Stretching also prevents the loss of flexibility and the pain and stiffness that make doing even simple activities difficult later in life. Unfortunately, flexibility is the most often overlooked part of an activity program.

ARE YOU FLEXIBLE ENOUGH?

Are your muscles and joints sore and stiff after yard work, exercise or recreational activities?	Yes	No
Are you sore and stiff first thing in the morning?	Yes	No
Do you feel less agile and flexible than you did a few years ago?	Yes	No
Does your range of motion seem limited when doing certain activities?	Yes	No

If you answered yes to any of these questions, you'll probably benefit from a program of regular stretching. Remember that flexibility is important for overall health and well-being too.

WHEN IS THE BEST TIME TO STRETCH?

Stretching should be done as part of your warm-up before and cooldown after physical activity. You may also want to do a routine program of stretching several times each week. In fact, stretching can be done anytime.

Guidelines for Safe Stretching
- Before stretching, warm up your body with 3 to 5 minutes of light activity.
- All stretches should be performed slowly and smoothly. Never bounce or jerk.
- Focus on the muscles and joints you're stretching and keep your body relaxed.
- Stretch to the point that you feel mild muscle tension. Don't stretch to the point of pain! Overstretching will do more harm than good.
- Hold each stretch for 15 to 20 seconds. Relax and breathe easily during each stretch. Never hold your breath.
- Avoid stretches that cause you to arch your back or neck backward or put stress on your knees.
- Don't do any stretch that could cause you to lose your balance and fall.
- Never compare yourself to others. Flexibility is not about how far you can stretch, it's about loosening and relaxing the muscles and joints.

STRETCHING EXERCISES

The following exercises are basic stretches for the major muscles and joints. Spend more time on your stiffest areas, but try to do all these stretches several times each week. You can do all the stretches at one time or do different stretches at different times of the day. The best way is to start with your neck and work your way down. Repeat each of the following stretches two to three times. Remember to relax, go slow and enjoy the time you spend stretching. Stretching is a great time to pray and meditate on Scripture.

Neck
These can be done sitting or standing.
- While looking straight ahead, tilt your head to the side as though you're trying to touch your ear to your shoulder. Hold the stretch for a few seconds; then repeat the movement to the other side.
- Next, try to touch your chin to your chest. Go down only as far as is comfortable, hold for a few seconds and take a deep breath. Return to the starting position.

Shoulders and Arms
These can be done sitting or standing.
- Reach up and over your head with one or both arms, as if trying to touch the ceiling. Bend slightly to each side. Repeat with the other arm.
- Next, reach forward with one arm and then stretch it across your chest toward the opposite shoulder. Increase the stretch by pulling with the opposite arm. Repeat with the other arm.
- Starting with your arms at your side, shrug your shoulders by bringing them up toward your ears. Lower your shoulders while stretching them backward, pulling the shoulder blades together. Return to the starting position with your arms at your sides.
- Hold your arms straight out to the side. Make wide circles with your arms, both forward and backward, by turning them at the shoulder. Make circles with your wrists too.

Trunk and Sides
- With your arms at your side and feet at least shoulder width apart, bend toward one side while sliding your arm down the side of your hip and leg. Stretch only as far as is comfortable and watch your balance. Keep your back and neck straight while doing this stretch. Repeat, this time stretching toward the other side.

Lower Back
- While sitting in a chair with your knees bent, bend forward from the waist and slide your hands down your legs toward your toes. Bend down only as far as is comfortable. Hold the stretch for a few seconds and rise back up slowly.
- Lie on your back with your knees bent and feet flat on the ground. Use your hands to pull one knee up toward the chest, while keeping your leg bent. As you pull up, press your back gently toward the floor. Keep the opposite leg bent at a 90-degree angle and your foot flat on the floor. Hold the stretch for a few seconds. Repeat with the other leg.
- Lie with your knees bent at a 90-degree angle and feet flat on the floor. Press the small of

your back toward the floor while tightening your stomach muscles. Hold the stretch for a few seconds.

- Kneel on your hands and knees and relax your neck. Arch your back up like a cat, feeling the stretch across your back. Hold for a few seconds. Repeat.

Legs and Ankles

- Sit on the floor. With your legs extended and your knees slightly bent, stretch forward at the waist and try to touch your toes. You don't have to touch your toes, just bend forward until you feel a stretch in the back of your legs. Keep your head and back as straight as possible and breathe easily.
- Face a wall with your arms extended straight out in front of you. Move one foot forward and leave the other foot back one to two feet. Keeping the heel of your back foot on the ground and toes pointing forward, lean your body toward the wall until you feel a mild stretch in your calf and heel. Hold the stretch for a few seconds. Repeat the stretch by changing the position of your feet.
- To loosen up your ankles, draw an imaginary circle with your foot by turning your foot at the ankle. Do circles in both directions. Repeat several times with each foot.

Health Assessment

UNDERSTANDING WEIGHT GAIN AND OBESITY—PART I
THE INCREASE IN BEING OVERWEIGHT

Despite an increasing emphasis on healthier lifestyles, the number of Americans who are overweight is growing rapidly. Currently one-half of adults are overweight or obese, and the degree of obesity in children is increasing at an even more rapid rate. At any one time, nearly 50 percent of men and women are trying to lose weight. Unfortunately, they are usually unsuccessful.

IS YOUR WEIGHT INCREASING?

How much weight have you gained in the past	1 year?	5 years?	10 years?

Has your weight been increasing steadily over the last several years? Or have you noticed a sudden jump in your weight? What changes in your life and lifestyle may be contributing to your weight gain? One of the best things you can do for your overall health is to prevent any further weight gain. In fact, studies show that following a healthy lifestyle of good nutrition and regular physical activity is more important to your overall health and well-being than what you weigh. Committing yourself to a healthy lifestyle and maintaining your present weight are important and worthwhile goals.

WHY THE INCREASE IN BEING OVERWEIGHT?

Most experts attribute increasing levels of obesity to the demands of modern living. Longer work hours and more time spent in the car leave less time for physical activity and healthy eating. It's not hard to see that remote controls, computers, self-propelled lawnmowers and drive-thrus have become part of everyday life. While modern technology is good, it decreases opportunities for physical activity at home and at work. Combined with easy access to a variety of high-calorie, high-fat and good-tasting foods, modern living makes it very difficult to maintain a healthy weight.

While weight gain results from an imbalance between calorie intake and energy expenditure, weight regulation is actually a complex process that involves physical, hormonal, environmental, genetic, emotional and social issues. These factors can all work together to influence metabolism, appetite, body composition, activity levels and lifestyle choices.

Society's view that obesity is an issue of willpower and choice, and popular diets that place the blame on certain foods or one specific cause, are overly simplistic and misleading.

Check any of the factors below that you feel have contributed to your weight gain.

- [ ] Stress
- [ ] Too busy
- [ ] Inactivity
- [ ] Genetics (obesity runs in my family)
- [ ] It's difficult to make healthy choices

- [ ] Emotional reasons
- [ ] I think I have a slow metabolism
- [ ] No one around me eats healthy or exercises
- [ ] I have a hard time controlling portion sizes
- [ ] Other _____

Prayerfully consider your life and lifestyle. Be honest as you ask yourself the following questions:

➻ Which factors are contributing to your present weight?

➻ What factors are in your control?

➻ Considering the fact that you are most likely to be successful in changing those aspects of your lifestyle that you're ready to change and that you're most confident you can change, what changes in your environment and lifestyle are you ready to make?

THE HEALTH RISKS OF BEING OVERWEIGHT

A lifestyle of poor dietary habits and physical inactivity, often resulting in becoming overweight or obese, is the second leading cause of preventable death in this country, resulting in over 300,000 deaths each year! Being overweight and obese are major risk factors for coronary heart disease and are strongly associated with several health problems, including:

Diabetes	Cancer	Gallbladder disease
High cholesterol	Stroke	Sleep problems
High blood pressure	Arthritis	Infertility

Good News!

Scientific evidence now shows that a weight loss of just 5 to 10 percent can significantly reduce—and even reverse!—the negative health effects associated with being overweight or obese. Moderate weight loss is also associated with an improved quality of life. With this new evidence, experts are abandoning the concept of "ideal" weight in favor of the term "healthier" weight.

➤ What are your health risks? Answer the following questions honestly.

Do you have any obesity-related diseases or health risks?	Yes	No
If so, list them here:		
If you don't know your risk factors, visit your doctor for a checkup.		
Because some diseases and risk factors don't develop until later in life, it's important to look at what problems run in your family. Do any obesity-related diseases or health risks run in your family?	Yes	No
If so, list them here:		
Do you believe that losing weight will help lower your risk factors?	Yes	No
Are you ready to commit to losing at least 10 percent of your current weight (if you're overweight) to improve your health?	Yes	No
Multiply your current body weight by .9 to determine your healthier weight	_____	
Are you willing to make the lifestyle changes necessary to achieve and maintain this weight, even if you can't achieve your ideal weight?	Yes	No

Losing weight and keeping it off are both difficult. Even the best weight-loss programs are associated with an average weight loss of only 10 to 15 percent—hardly enough to reach the ideal most of us would like! In fact, 60 percent of people who are initially successful in losing weight gain it back within a year; almost all gain it back within three to five years! Are your expectations realistic? Be careful not to set weight and lifestyle goals that you cannot realistically keep.

UNDERSTANDING WEIGHT GAIN AND OBESITY—PART II
UNDERSTANDING YOUR HEALTHY WEIGHT

Many people have unrealistic expectations about their bodies and ideal body weight. We live in a society that values a lean and fit body, but a healthy weight is not necessarily the popular ideal. More important is living a healthy lifestyle and maintaining a weight that's associated with good health and abundant living (see John 10:10). A healthy weight considers who you are emotionally, spiritually, intellectually, physically and socially. Your goal should be to follow a lifestyle that's in balance with God's overall desire for your life (see Mark 12:30,31).

WHAT *IS* YOUR HEALTHY WEIGHT?

In Part I you learned about the health risks of being overweight and obese. You also learned about the importance of reaching and maintaining your healthier weight. This worksheet will give you some additional tools to help you set goals and track your progress.

Experts now use Body Mass Index (BMI) to determine healthy weight. The healthy weight range you determined in the Finding Your Healthy Weight worksheet (pp. 34-36) is based on BMI. A healthy weight is not about physical appearance or a number on the scale. In most people, BMI provides an accurate reflection of body composition and health risks.

HOW TO CALCULATE YOUR BMI

Multiply your current weight in pounds by 703

Weight _____ x 703 = (a) _____

Divide the result (a) by your height in inches

(a) _____ ÷ height _____ = (b) _____

Divide the result (b) by your height in inches

(b) _____ ÷ height _____ = BMI _____

Understanding Your BMI

< 21	— Weight loss not indicated
21 to 25	— This is your healthy weight range
26 to 30	— Increasing health risk
> 30	— Obesity and high health risk
> 40	— Very high health risk

Note: Some people who are very muscular and fit can have a high BMI yet be very lean and healthy.

ARE YOU AN APPLE OR A PEAR?

Where you carry your weight is also related to the health risks associated with obesity. People who tend to put on weight above the waist—those who are apple shaped—have a greater chance of developing heart disease, abnormal cholesterol levels, high blood pressure and diabetes. People who carry their extra weight below the waistline—pear shaped—don't seem to have as high a risk of developing these conditions. To find out your shape and determine your risk, you can measure your waist and hips to determine your waist-to-hip ratio.

HOW TO DETERMINE YOUR WAIST-TO-HIP RATIO

- Measure around the smallest part of your waistline in inches; don't pull in, just stand relaxed. The narrowest part of your waistline is usually at the level of your hipbone and near your belly button.
- Next, measure your hips in inches at the widest part of your buttocks.
- Divide your waist measurement by your hip measurement:

  Waist _____ ÷ hip _____ = waist-to-hip ratio _____

  A healthy waist-to-hip ratio for women is below .8 and for men below 1.0.

KNOW YOUR WAIST SIZE

Your waist size is also a good measure of the amount of fat you carry in your abdomen. Some experts feel that waist size is a better indicator of health risk than the waist-to-hip ratio. A waist measurement greater than 35 inches for women and 40 inches for men indicate a much higher risk of developing weight-related health problems. Because the scale doesn't always reflect what's happening to your body weight, pay attention to your waistline. Are your clothes fitting differently? Is your waistline getting smaller? These are often better indicators of healthy weight loss than following the numbers on the scale.

AVOIDING THE YO-YO EFFECT

Healthy weight loss also involves achieving a weight and following a lifestyle that you can maintain for a lifetime. Repeated cycles of weight loss and weight gain—yo-yo dieting—are not healthy. It's important to set realistic goals. Unrealistic goals and expectations encourage unhealthy weight-loss methods, result in yo-yo dieting and set you up for failure and discouragement. It's better to achieve and maintain moderate weight loss than it is to cycle repeatedly, losing and gaining large amounts of weight. Repeated ups and downs—both on the scale and emotionally—are not the answer for good health and abundant living.

To be successful in losing weight and maintaining it for a lifetime, it's important to examine your past attempts to lose weight. How many times have you lost

10 lbs.?   20 lbs.?   30 lbs.?   40 lbs.?   50 lbs.?   +50 lbs.?

What's the longest period of time you've been able to maintain a significant weight loss?

Looking back at past attempts to lose weight, determine which things worked and which didn't. How ready are you to lose weight this time compared to previous attempts? Are you willing and ready to make a commitment to the permanent lifestyle changes necessary for good health and long-term weight loss?

Unrealistic or Negative Feelings About Your Body

Are you dissatisfied with your body and its shape? Do you worry a lot about your appearance? Remember that you are fearfully and wonderfully made (see Psalm 139:14). God values your heart. Don't let the unrealistic expectations of others influence how you think about yourself. Let God, who knows and loves you, and your own heartfelt sense of who you are determine your value and what weight is right for you.

> Be honest in your estimate of yourselves, measuring your value by how much faith God has given you (Romans 12:3, *TLB*).

Unrealistic goals and expectations about weight loss and body image can lead to feelings of guilt, failure and disappointment. Prayerfully consider your thoughts and feelings about your weight. By taking your focus off the scale, you can commit yourself better to a healthy lifestyle of good nutrition and regular physical activity. The benefits of a healthy lifestyle include a greater sense of well-being, more energy and more effective living.

➤ What are your reasons for wanting to lose weight?

UNDERSTANDING WEIGHT GAIN AND OBESITY—PART III
ACHIEVING AND MAINTAINING WEIGHT LOSS

Hopefully, with the help of Parts I and II of this series you've been able to gain some important insights about your weight, how you feel about your body and how to set realistic and achievable goals. Remember, this is only the beginning. Once you achieve your goals of a healthy weight, you can set new goals if you desire. Many First Place members have healthfully lost large amounts of weight. Unfortunately, many people also abandon their efforts because of their inability to meet unrealistic goals and expectations.

To lose weight healthfully and successfully, you can use several important tools. Review the following strategies and find ways to incorporate them into your plan.

THE IMPORTANCE OF PHYSICAL ACTIVITY

Weight gain and obesity are often viewed as problems of eating too much. While this is part of the problem, obesity is just as likely to result from too little physical activity. Many experts feel that the alarming increase in being overweight and obese discussed in Part 1 of this series is a result of the sedentary lifestyles of most Americans. Today nearly 25 percent of Americans are completely sedentary, and up to 60 percent do not get enough physical activity to benefit their health. Increasing physical activity—energy expenditure—is as important to weight control as decreasing calorie intake.

What the Research Shows
An important study published in the *American Journal of Clinical Nutrition* surveyed nearly 800 men and women from the National Weight Control Registry who maintained an average weight loss of more than 60 pounds for over 5 years. In this survey, 90 percent of the participants reported regular physical activity as a part of their program. Other studies have reported similar findings.

A series of studies reported by researchers from the Cooper Institute for Aerobics Research in Dallas, Texas, reveal that death rates from all causes are much lower in obese men with a moderate to high level of physical fitness than in normal-weight men with low physical fitness. These important studies confirm that a lifestyle of physical activity and healthy eating is more important than the number on the scale. In other words, as the researchers from this study reported: "It's better to be fit and fat than lean and sedentary."

The Benefits of Physical Activity
- Helps the body burn fat and protects against the muscle loss associated with low-calorie eating plans
- Helps the body maintain or increase its metabolic rate
- May help suppress appetite

- Allows for weight loss on a higher calorie eating plan, which helps the body get all the nutrients it needs
- Improves mood and self-esteem
- Results in important health benefits such as lower blood pressure, improved cholesterol levels and increased fitness
- Promotes long-term weight maintenance

MORE STRATEGIES FOR SUCCESSFUL WEIGHT LOSS

Self-Monitoring Using the Commitment Record

Studies confirm that one of the most effective factors in weight loss is keeping a food and activity diary. Use your Commitment Record (CR) to help you keep track of what you eat and why you eat. In other words, your CR is not just for recording information; it's also for observing and evaluating your habits, moods and choices. Reviewing your CR regularly can help you prepare for situations and feelings that make it difficult for you to stick with your plan. Many successful First Place members report that keeping their CR is the most important reason for their success. Keeping a weight chart and other important health information is also important in monitoring your progress.

Have you been making the most of your CR? Don't underestimate the value of this important tool!

Get the Support of Family and Friends

Support of family and friends helps promote success for many people. Surround yourself with people who can help provide you with the positive support and encouragement you need for success.

It's also important to look out for people who can sabotage your efforts. Do you know people who continually offer you food, encourage you to eat less healthy foods, interfere with your physical activity or find other ways to try to derail your efforts to lose weight and eat more healthy?

Take some time to consider some ways family and friends can help you reach your goals. Make a plan to ask them for the specific help you need. It's also important to recognize those people who make it difficult for you to reach your goals.

➢ What steps can you take to avoid these negative influences?

Learn to Manage Your Stress

Emotional and physical stress can make it difficult to stick with a healthy lifestyle. Dealing with stress appropriately through prayer, biblical meditation, social support, relaxation exercises and other coping techniques can help you stick with your plan and achieve your goals.

Is stress a factor in your life at this time? Does stress influence your ability to make healthy choices and reach your goals? If you answered yes to these questions, read Matthew 6:25-34 and Philippians 4:4-7. Give your worries to God.

➤ What can you do today to lessen the effects of stress on your life?

Learn to Reward Yourself

Changing your lifestyle and losing weight are not easy tasks. It's important to reward yourself for your achievements. Every positive step you make—no matter how big or small—is important. Ask others to help you plan for special rewards as you reach your goals. Of course, the best rewards are those that motivate you from the inside. Learn to feel good about your accomplishments.

Do you enjoy your new lifestyle? Do you have more energy? Do you feel better? These are the best kinds of rewards. Rewards such as a new outfit or a special night out can also be helpful. Be careful not to reward yourself with too much food!

Learn to Deal With Setbacks

You *will* have setbacks and slipups (see 1 Corinthians 10:13). The key to successful weight loss is to see these as learning opportunities and not failures. Starting with reasonable goals and expectations is the best way to keep setbacks from becoming complete failures. Avoid absolutes such as *never, always, must* and *should*. Slipups will happen; learn to forgive yourself and move on. Think about some situations in the past when you have allowed one slipup to knock you off your program.

➤ What can you do differently this time?

UNDERSTANDING YOUR EATING HABITS

Habits are difficult to change. However, you must change your habits to achieve your goals for a healthy weight and good nutrition. Successful change requires that you identify those habits that are keeping you from achieving your goals. It's also important to recognize those things you do well. Most people are in such a hurry to reach their goals that they fail to make a plan they can stick with for the long haul. It's better to spend several weeks learning about yourself and making a plan than it is to jump immediately into a program that you can't stick with.

Work through the following Eating Habits Inventory to help you understand yourself and what circumstances make it difficult for you to reach and maintain your goals. The inventory will also help you identify those habits that you need to change. After completing the inventory, review your habits and then focus on those habits that you're most ready to change. Use it to help you develop a plan that's right for you. Review your inventory often to help you monitor your progress and adjust your plan.

EATING HABITS INVENTORY

Understanding what foods you eat and how they influence your goals for achieving and maintaining a healthy weight will help you build a plan for successful change.

➤ Are you in control when it comes to eating?

➤ Is it easy for you to make healthy choices?

➤ Does stress, loneliness or an argument with a loved one cause you to overeat?

➤ In what situations are you most likely to lose control?

➤ Do you have plans to help you overcome difficult situations?

➤ What foods do you eat that are consistent with your goals for a healthy weight and good nutrition?

➤ What foods do you eat frequently that keep you from reaching your goals?

➤ What foods do you need to eat more often to help you reach your goals?

Now that you've thought about the foods you eat, it's important to understand that you have control over several factors that influence the choices you make.

- What foods you buy at the grocery store
- How you plan and prepare meals at home
- The situations, people and feelings that influence the foods you eat
- What choices you make when you eat away from home: restaurants, work, social occasions, etc.
- The variety of foods you choose to eat throughout the day

➤ What changes are you most ready to make when it comes to the foods you eat?

➤ When and where do you most often eat?

Do you...		
Eat at regular times each day?	Yes	No
Eat three meals each day?	Yes	No
Skip meals regularly? If yes, which one(s)? _____	Yes	No
Often wait too long between meals (six or more hours)?	Yes	No
Often eat more than you want (i.e., beyond the point of being comfortably full)?	Yes	No
Overeat when you're around your favorite foods?	Yes	No
Often eat second helpings?	Yes	No
Eat too rapidly (i.e., meals in less than 20 minutes or snacks in less than 10 minutes)?	Yes	No
Eat in a place other than the dining room or at the kitchen table?	Yes	No
Eat while cooking or cleaning up?	Yes	No
Do you eat while watching television, talking on the telephone or doing other activities?	Yes	No

THE IMPORTANCE OF EATING REGULAR MEALS

It's important to eat at least three regular meals each day. Your body needs fuel and a variety of nutrients throughout the day. Regular meals keep your body's tank full. Skipping meals makes it harder for you to get the nutrition you need. For example, several studies indicate that breakfast eaters are healthier and eat more nutritiously throughout the day compared to those who skip breakfast. Some experts believe that eating regular meals is also better for your body's metabolism. It's much easier to maintain your healthy habits when you stay on a regular schedule.

Healthy snacking is also an important part of an eating plan for weight loss. A regular snack can help maintain your energy levels and curb your appetite to prevent overeating at other meals. Keep your snack times consistent and have a plan for what you will eat. Keep healthy snack foods available.

CONTROL THE AMOUNT YOU EAT

Slow Down!
A good way to control the amount you eat is to slow down. The slower you eat, the less likely you are to overeat and the more you'll enjoy your food. Experts estimate that it takes 20 minutes for your body to tell your brain that you've had enough to eat. Slow down and listen to your body's natural hunger signals.

Cut Down!
Continually put your knowledge of portion sizes to work for you. If you're not achieving your weight-loss goals, review your portion sizes. Serve smaller meals and don't go back for seconds unless you're truly hungry. Have a plan for when you know you will be eating your favorite foods. Limit yourself to smaller portions and eat more slowly so that you enjoy each bite. It's important to learn to stop eating when you're no longer hungry.

Sit Down!
It's easy to take in hidden calories if you're not paying attention to what or where you're eating. Try to have only one or two places in the house where you eat. For example, eat only while you are sitting at the dinner table. Don't eat while you're doing other activities such as cooking, watching television or talking on the telephone.

LEARN TO EAT HEALTHY AT EVERY MEAL

⮞ What changes are you most ready to make to your eating habits?

⮞ Circle the meal that applies to each of the following questions:

What is your most healthy meal of the day?

Breakfast   Lunch   Dinner   Between-meal snacks

What is your least healthy meal of the day?

Breakfast   Lunch   Dinner   Between-meal snacks

➤ What's different about your least healthy meal compared to your most healthy meal of the day?

➤ Why is it more difficult to make healthy choices during one meal and not another?

➤ Is it where you eat or what you eat that's causing the problem? Or is it who you eat with?

➤ Are you better prepared to eat healthy at one meal compared to another? Which one?

➤ What habits can you change to begin making better choices for your least healthy meal of the day?

EATING OUT

Where are you most likely to eat out?

1.

2.

3.

4.

➤ When you eat at these restaurants, are you more or less likely to make choices that will help you reach your goals?

➤ In what situations do you tend to make less healthy choices or eat more than you need (e.g., when you eat out, at parties, buffets or other social events)?

Choose two or three restaurants where you know you can make healthy choices. Learn the menu and become comfortable with making special requests. You don't have to avoid your favorite restaurants completely. Just make sure you have a plan for making good choices. Other tips for eating out include controlling your portion sizes, sharing your meal with a companion, using a to-go box and making healthy choices throughout the rest of the day.

Special occasions such as parties, meetings or eating out with friends often trigger overeating and poor choices. It's very important to be aware of the situations that are most likely to make it difficult for you to make healthy choices. Have a plan to help keep you on track. Consider some of the following suggestions:

- Eat a healthy snack or exercise before going out.
- Keep healthy foods with you so you have another option when presented with foods not on your plan.
- Learn to say, "No, thank you."
- Learn to eat smaller portions and to stop eating when you are full.
- Rehearse special situations in your mind and pray about them ahead of time so you'll be ready to make the right choices when you're there.
- Make your priority talking with others rather than eating.
- Stay away from areas at parties or in buffet lines that will tempt you.

➤ What changes are you most ready to make to your eating habits?

➤ With whom do you eat?

➤ Which people are most likely to influence the choices you make?

➤ Do you tend to eat more food when alone or with others?

➻ Which people have the most positive influence on what you eat?

➻ Which people have the most negative influence on what you eat?

It's important to understand what relationships help or hurt your ability to make good choices. Ask people to give you the specific help you need. Surround yourself with people who are most likely to encourage you to make good choices. Find ways to avoid situations that make it difficult for you to make good decisions. Don't let others keep you from achieving and maintaining your goal.

➻ What can you do to get the support you need from family and friends?

➻ Why do you eat?

Usually we eat because we're hungry. Sometimes we eat for fun and fellowship. We also eat for other reasons. Do your moods affect what you eat? If yes, which moods influence you the most? Check below.

☐ Loneliness ☐ Anger ☐ Fatigue ☐ Excitement
☐ Depression ☐ Sadness ☐ Anxiety ☐ Other _____
☐ Stress ☐ Happiness ☐ Boredom ☐ Other _____

What are the most important factors that contribute to your being overweight, make it difficult for you to achieve or maintain your healthy weight or make it difficult for you to eat healthy? Check below.

☐ I generally eat too much.   ☐ My emotions often influence what I eat.
☐ I often eat when I'm not hungry.   ☐ I eat out too much.
☐ I don't get enough physical activity.   ☐ I enjoy eating.
☐ I eat too many sweets or fattening foods. ☐ I don't have enough time to eat right.
☐ I eat too many snacks.   ☐ I don't want to give up foods I enjoy.
☐ Other_____   ☐ Other_____

>> Are you an emotional eater? What are some positive ways you can deal with your emotions?

Learn to avoid negative, or all-or-nothing, thinking: *I've blown it now; I might as well give up.* Substitute positive thoughts and activities for negative emotions. Talk to family or friends to get a better understanding of those situations and emotions that are most difficult for you. Take time to consider your emotions prayerfully.

>> Why do you allow your emotions to influence how you take care of yourself?

Read, meditate on or recite encouraging and supportive Scripture. Respond to your emotions by doing other positive activities like listening to music or being physically active.

>> How can you begin to deal with your emotions more effectively?

PUTTING IT ALL TOGETHER

After reviewing your Eating Habits Inventory, begin to make a plan for change. Focus on both your good and bad habits. For example, if you're eating lots of fruits and vegetables, that's great! Use your good habits to help you take positive steps in other areas. However, to achieve and maintain your goals for a healthy weight and good nutrition, you must focus most of your attention on those habits you need to change.

Use the following suggestions to help you build a plan that's best for you:

- What habits are you most ready to change?
- What habits are you most confident you can change?
- What information, support and plans do you need to begin making these changes?
- Commit yourself to a specific plan for change.
- Remember, change is best made through a series of small steps. Make sure you feel good about each step you take and reward yourself along the way.
- Review your habits and your plans regularly so you can monitor your progress. When you experience difficulty and challenges, change your plans rather than abandoning your program.

KEYS TO SUCCESSFUL LIFESTYLE CHANGE

- A meaningful purpose that provides the right motivation for change
- Realistic and flexible goals
- A well thought-out plan
- Supportive relationships
- A willingness to accept mistakes and learn from them
- Regular monitoring of progress
- A positive attitude
- A life centered in faith, prayer, worship and fellowship

Nutrition

WHAT'S THE BIG DEAL ABOUT WATER?

You've probably heard more than once that you should drink eight 8-ounce glasses of water each day. Why the fuss? For starters, water makes up about 80 percent of your muscle mass, 60 percent of your red blood cells and more than 90 percent of your blood plasma. If you were stranded on a deserted island, you could go for weeks without food but only a few days without water. Take a look at the important role water plays in your body:

- It aids in the digestion and absorption of foods and nutrients.
- Water helps regulate the chemical reactions in every cell of your body.
- It transports nutrients and oxygen.
- Water is the vehicle your body uses to flush out the waste produced in normal body functions.
- It helps you maintain normal body temperature.
- Water is necessary for proper bowel function.
- It is responsible for maintaining proper fluid balance.

In your quest for healthy living, drinking plenty of water should be a top priority. In fact, if you're currently not drinking enough water, doing so will be one of the most significant lifestyle changes you can make.

WHY CHOOSE WATER?

All fluids and some foods count toward your daily total of water. So why choose water? Water is good for you, it contains no calories, it's low in sodium, and it contains no additives or stimulants. Substituting water for calorie-containing beverages is an important step in helping you achieve and maintain a healthy body weight. Nonfat milk and 100 percent fruit juices are also good choices—they're packed with vitamins and minerals. However, watch the calories. The caffeine in tea, soft drinks and coffee acts as a stimulant and a diuretic (i.e., causes your body to lose water); thus, caffeine is not a good choice. Choose God's abundant water as your number one beverage!

Your body loses about 8 to 12 ounces of water throughout the day. To stay healthy and feel your best, you need to replace what your body loses. There's nothing magical about eight glasses of water a day; some people need a little more, some a little less. Drinking water throughout the day helps keep you ahead of the game.

TAP OR BOTTLED?

Americans drink about 3.4 billion gallons of bottled water each year, and the numbers have been increasing about 10 percent per year. If drinking water from a bottle will encourage you to drink more, then bottled water is a good choice. However, don't assume that it's purer than tap water. In fact, according to the Natural Resources Defense Council (NRDC), some bottled waters may not be any better than tap water; they may even *be* tap water! In a recent study, the group found that one-third of 103 tested brands contained bacteria or other chemicals that exceed the industry's own guidelines or state purity standards.

While bottled water is safe, the NRDC noted that bottled-water companies tout the health benefits of their products and that consumers should be getting their money's worth. Since the study was released, legislation has been proposed for stricter standards on bottled water. Tap water is regulated under provisions of the Safe Drinking Water Act of 1974.

EIGHT GLASSES A DAY? THAT'S IMPOSSIBLE!

Once you start drinking more water, your natural thirst for it will increase. With each glass you drink, think about the physical benefits. From time to time, review the list at the beginning of this worksheet that details how important water is to your body.

To make drinking water a habit, start by filling an eight-ounce measuring cup with water. Eight ounces is probably not as much as you think. What size glass will you use for those eight ounces? Another tactic is to fill a two-quart (64 ounce) container with water each morning and by noon make sure you have only one quart left. You're halfway to your goal!

You can keep a two-quart pitcher of water on your desk or in your refrigerator for easy access to water. Additionally, keep a water bottle in your car, take it to meetings and be sure to have water available when you exercise.

Some ways to make water more tantalizing:

- Fill a pitcher with water, and add several orange slices for a light, refreshing flavor.
- Always ask for water when dining out, and try adding lemon or lime slices.
- Choose sparkling waters.

DEHYDRATION

During the summer, you require more water because your body loses water through perspiration. If you live in a dry climate, your perspiration may evaporate more quickly so you might not sense the need to drink water, even though your body is still losing fluids. Don't wait for perspiration to be your warning sign to consume more water. The dry air in winter also increases your body's need for water. Don't wait until you feel thirsty to drink water; stay ahead of your thirst.

In addition to thirst, early signs of dehydration include the following:

- Fatigue
- Loss of appetite
- Flushed skin
- Light-headedness and dizziness
- Muscle cramping
- Infrequent urination and urine that's dark yellow

WATER AND PHYSICAL ACTIVITY

During physical activity, pay close attention to your water intake. Make sure you drink at least eight ounces before activity, and every 15 to 20 minutes during activity. You may need more when it's hot outside. To find out how much water you need to replenish your exercise losses, weigh yourself before and after exercise—the difference is mainly water. Replace one pound of weight loss with 16 ounces of water.

While the number on the scale may look better, dehydration is not a healthy way to lose weight. Avoid using sweatsuits or rubberized clothing to increase sweating during exercise. This is a dangerous practice and the weight you lose is only water—not fat! Body fat is made up of only 25 percent water compared to almost 80 percent water in muscle. Dehydration robs your body of the water it needs.

Unless you are an endurance athlete training for more than an hour, drink water rather than sports drinks.

AN ESSENTIAL NUTRIENT

While water is not included on the Food Guide Pyramid, don't ignore its importance. Next to air, you need water most for survival. Keep well hydrated and your body will perform better than ever. And you'll feel great too!

UNDERSTANDING THE NUTRITION FACTS PANEL

You don't need a degree in nutrition or chemistry to eat healthy. The nutrition facts panel gives you all you need to know. Learning to read labels can help you choose the foods that best fit into your Live-It plan. The nutrition facts panel provides information on calories, fat, saturated fat, cholesterol, fiber and other important nutrients in a single serving. The ingredients list tells you what's in a food, with ingredients listed from most to least. Food labels can also include nutrition and health claims.

SERVING SIZE

The serving size is based on a typical portion, not necessarily the recommended serving. Compare the serving size on the panel with the exchange for that food. Is it more or less? How does the serving size compare to what you eat? Controlling serving size is the best way to make your Live-It plan work for you.

% DAILY VALUE

The % daily value shows how one serving counts toward the recommended daily intake for specific nutrients. The percentage is based on a 2,000-calorie diet. Use the % daily value to see if a food is high or low in specific nutrients.

CALORIES

How does the calorie level compare to what you know about the calorie exchange for that food? Calories from fat is the *number* of calories from fat, *not* the percentage. If you want to determine the percentage, divide the calories from fat by the calories. On average, choose more foods with 30 percent or less of calories from fat. Not every food you eat has to be less than 30 percent fat—just the overall balance of foods you eat!

NUTRIENTS

Total fat, saturated fat, cholesterol, sodium, carbohydrates, fiber, sugars, protein, vitamins A and C, calcium and iron must be listed on the label. Vitamins and minerals added to foods must also be listed.

For total fat, saturated fat, cholesterol and sodium, look for foods with a low percent daily value.

For vitamins, minerals and fiber, your goal is to reach a 100 percent each day. Choose foods with a high percentage of nutrients; a good source contains 10 percent or more.

At the bottom of the panel is the recommended amount of important nutrients for a 2,000 and a 2,500 calorie diet. It shows the maximum amounts of total fat, saturated fat, cholesterol and sodium recommended for a healthy and balanced eating plan: no more than 30 percent calories from fat, less than 10 percent saturated fat and less than 60 percent of total calories from carbohydrates. The last item on the panel is the number of calories per gram of fat, carbohydrate and protein.

USING THE LABEL TO FIGURE OUT EXCHANGES

The nutrition facts panel gives you all you need to know to figure out the exchanges for a typical serving of any food: total calories and grams of fat, protein and carbohydrate. Be sure to adjust the calorie and nutrient amounts if you're eating more or less than one serving. Some food labels even provide the exchanges. If not, you can call the manufacturer or distributor and ask for the exchanges for that food. Most labels list the phone number and address you can call for information.

UNDERSTANDING NUTRITION AND HEALTH CLAIMS

When it comes to health and nutrition claims, you can believe what you read. Food makers must meet strict government guidelines to list terms such as "low fat" or "reduced-sodium" or to make health claims about heart disease, cancer or other diseases. Only health claims that are supported by scientific evidence and approved by the Food and Drug Administration (FDA) are allowed.

Understanding Terms	
Calorie free	Fewer than 5 calories in a serving
Low calorie	40 calories or less in a serving
Fat free	Less than 1/2 (0.5) gram of total fat in a serving
Low fat	3 grams or less of total fat in a serving
Saturated fat free	Less than 1/2 gram saturated fat in a serving
Low saturated fat	1 gram saturated fat or less in a serving
Cholesterol free	Less than 2 milligrams cholesterol and 2 grams or less saturated fat in a serving
Low cholesterol	20 milligrams or less cholesterol and 2 grams or less saturated fat in a serving
Sodium free	Fewer than 5 milligrams sodium in a serving
Low sodium	140 milligrams sodium or less in a serving
Very low sodium	35 milligrams or less in a serving
Sugar free	Less than 0.5 grams sugar in a serving
Light or lite	1/3 less calories or 50 percent less of a nutrient such as fat, sodium or sugar than the regular or reference food
Reduced	25 percent less calories, fat, saturated fat, cholesterol, sodium or sugar than the regular or reference food; words such as "lower" and "fewer" might also be used.

Understanding Terms (continued)	
Lean	Fewer than 10 grams fat, 4.5 grams or less saturated fat and less than 95 milligrams cholesterol in a serving
Extra lean	Fewer than 5 grams fat, less than 2 grams saturated fat and less than 95 milligrams cholesterol in a serving
High	20 percent or more of % Daily Value for a nutrient such as a vitamin, mineral, or fiber; "excellent source of" and "rich in" may also be used.
Good source	10 to 19 percent of the % Daily Value for a nutrient
More	10 percent or more of the % Daily Value for a nutrient; "enriched," "fortified" and "added" might also be used.
Healthy	Low in fat and saturated fat, 480 milligrams or fewer of sodium and at least 10 percent of the % Daily Value of vitamin A, vitamin C, calcium, iron, protein and fiber in a serving

SUGAR: SWEETNESS BY ANY OTHER NAME

Many different sugars are found naturally in foods. Sugars are also added in the preparation and manufacturing of many foods. In addition to tasting good, sugar plays several important roles in food. It gives certain foods their characteristic texture, color and consistency. You may have discovered the difference sugar makes when you reduce or substitute it in recipes.

Myths and misinformation about sugar and other sweeteners are very common. Common table sugar, or refined sugar, tops the misinformation list. You've probably also heard stories about saccharin and aspartame. Whether the sugar comes from the sugar bowl, honey, fruit, vegetables or milk, there's little difference from your body's viewpoint. In the end, your body converts sugars and starches from fruits, vegetables, grains and other foods to glucose. Along with fatty acids (fat), glucose is the main energy source for your body.

HOW DOES IT STACK UP?

A gram of sugar contains four calories. That's less than half of the nine calories supplied by a gram of fat. A teaspoon of sugar contains 16 calories. A soft drink can have 9 to 12 teaspoons of sugar! What's the real problem? The estimated 150 pounds of sugar that the average American consumes each year adds up to a lot of calories. The bottom line is that too many calories are fattening, and it doesn't really matter whether the extra calories come from sugars, fat or protein. We gain weight when we take in more calories from our food than we expend in physical activity. The problem with sugar is that it often supplies empty calories (i.e., calories without the nutrition). Sugar is also often found in foods that are high in calories and fat. Because most of us have a sweet tooth, sugary foods often replace other more nutritious foods in our diets.

WHAT'S IN A NAME?

Sweeteners have many names. Check the following that you recognize.

☐ Acesulfame K	☐ Glucose	☐ Maple syrup
☐ Aspartame	☐ High fructose corn syrup	☐ Molasses
☐ Brown sugar	☐ Honey	☐ Saccharin
☐ Corn sweeteners	☐ Lactose	☐ Sorbitol
☐ Dextrose	☐ Maltose	☐ Sugar
☐ Fruit juice concentrate	☐ Mannitol	☐ Xylitol

While there are some minor differences, your body treats these sugars much the same. In terms of nutritional value there's virtually no difference. The nonnutritive sweeteners—acesulfame K, aspartame and saccharin—add sweetness without the calories.

What's on the Label?

Sugar-free	Less than 0.5 grams of sugar per serving
Reduced sugar	At least 25 percent less sugar per serving than the original product
No added sugar	No sugars added during processing or packaging

Note: Read the label—many sugar-free foods contain a sugar substitute such as aspartame.

How Sweet It Is!

Nonnutritive sweeteners (also known as artificial, or intense, sweeteners) can give you the taste of sugar without the calories. Even though foods made with nonnutritive sweeteners may be low in calories, many of them may also be low in nutrition. In a healthy eating plan, calories are not the only issue—you need to consider nutrition (i.e., vitamins, minerals, phytochemicals and fiber).

Four artificial sweeteners are commonly used today: aspartame, acesulfame potassium, saccharin and sucralose.

- **Aspartame**. Aspartame (NutraSweet, Equal) is a newer nonnutritive sweetener that actually contains calories. Because it's 180 times as sweet as sugar, you need only a tiny amount to sweeten food. It's actually a combination of two amino acids. One problem with aspartame is that it loses its sweetness when heated. Consequently, you cannot use it in baked goods, such as cakes. You can use it in top-of-the-stove foods like pudding by adding it at the very end of cooking. Available scientific evidence does not support various health concerns reported by some individuals.

- **Acesulfame Potassium**. Acesulfame potassium (Sunett) is 200 times sweeter than sugar and was first approved in 1988 as a tabletop sweetener. It is now approved for products such as baked goods, frozen desserts, candies and beverages. More than 90 studies verify its safety. It is often combined with other sweeteners. Worldwide, the sweetener is used in more than 4,000 products, according to its manufacturer, Nutrinova. It has excellent shelf life and does not break down when cooked or baked.

- **Saccharin**. Saccharin (Sweet 'N Low) has been around for over 100 years. It's over 300 times sweeter than table sugar—a little goes a long way! Saccharin can be used in both hot and cold foods to make them sweeter. Substituting saccharin for sugar in baked goods may change their taste, texture and appearance. The risk of cancer associated with the use of saccharin in laboratory animals appears to be very low or nonexistent in humans.

- **Sucralose**. Sucralose (Splenda) is 600 times sweeter than sugar. It was approved in 1998 as a tabletop sweetener and for use in products such as baked goods, beverages, gum, frozen dairy desserts, fruit juices and gelatins. It is now approved as a general purpose sweetener for all foods. It is bulked up with maltodextrin, a starchy powder, so it will measure more like sugar. It has a good shelf life and doesn't degrade when exposed to heat.

The key with both sugars and nonnutritive sweeteners is moderation. Let your overall goals of achieving and maintaining a healthy weight and good health help you decide what is best for you.

CAN YOU MAINTAIN YOUR EATING PLAN FOR A LIFETIME?

Moderation, balance and variety are the keys to achieving and maintaining a healthy weight and good nutrition. Some dietitians actually advise people who are trying to lose weight to include some sugary foods in their diets. Eating plans that restrict certain foods are often too hard to maintain. Trying to eliminate certain foods often leads to an eventual slipup (i.e., you break down and eat that food). Slipups often lead to feelings of guilt and failure. The feelings cause many people to abandon their weight-loss efforts. Others report that there are certain foods they need to avoid in order to achieve their goals. If eating some sugary foods allows you to better reach your goals, that's okay. If eliminating sugary foods or using nonnutritive sweeteners helps you reach your goals, that's okay too! Many members of First Place have found success with this last approach. You decide what's best for you and your body.

There are no good or bad foods, only bad diets. Your eating plan should not focus on what you're eliminating but what you're adding—good nutrition, improved health and a higher quality of life.

THE ANYTIME, ANYWHERE RESTAURANT GUIDE

Eating out is a great way to spend time with family and friends and enjoy good food. Believe it or not, you can dine out without blowing it! The key is having a plan for healthy eating and sticking with it.

➼ List four reasons you eat out.

1.

2.

3.

4.

➼ Do these reasons influence your ability to make healthy decisions? Is health or good nutrition on your list?

CHECK OUT WHAT'S ON THE MENU

Menus are full of food clues if you know what to look for. Here's a list of terms often used in menus:

Less Fat	More Fat
Baked or broiled	Fried
Poached	Breaded
Grilled	Sautéed (in butter or oil)
Tomato sauce	Alfredo or cream sauce
Roasted	Casserole
Steamed	Prime

- Choose single items and side dishes rather than complete meals.
- Ask for a to-go box before you eat your meal. Choose what you need and immediately box the rest.
- Share a dish with a companion or plan to eat smaller portions of dishes that are higher in calories, fat and sugar.

HEALTHY CHOICES FOR ANY MEAL

A Healthy Start

- Choose toast, small (or half) bagel or English muffin with a small amount of margarine or low-fat cream cheese and jam or jelly. Add nonfat milk and fruit or fruit juice to balance out your meal.
- Cold or hot cereals with nonfat milk are a great start to any day. Top with fresh or dried fruit for added nutrition. Choose wholesome cereals with little or no added sugar and three or more grams of fiber.
- Limit eggs (two or three each week), bacon, sausage, fried potatoes, biscuits, croissants and sweet rolls. Muffins can be high in calories, fat and sugar.

Midday Munching

- Broth-based soups and fresh salads with dressing on the side make a great noontime choice. Watch out for cream-based soups and potato, macaroni, tuna or chicken salads which are made with mayonnaise.
- Choose sandwiches with grilled chicken, lean roast beef, turkey or ham. Some deli-style sandwiches pack on the meat; ask for more vegetables instead. Order mustard or low-fat spreads instead of mayonnaise.
- Limit French fries, onion rings and chips. Ask that they be left off your plate or substitute a baked potato, fruit or vegetables. Burgers and hot dogs are okay occasionally, but avoid the deluxe versions.

A Night Out

- Choose baked, broiled or grilled chicken (without the skin), fish or small portions of other lean meats. Limit fried and prime cuts of meat and heavy sauces.
- Pastas with tomato-based sauces and fresh vegetables are good choices. Limit cream- or cheese-based sauces. When you do order them, ask that they be served on the side.
- Start your meal with a fresh salad and broth-based soup to help control your appetite. Better yet, when you know you are dining out, eat a piece of fruit or drink a glass of non-fat milk before you go.

Satisfy Your Sweet Tooth

- First, ask yourself if you're really hungry. If you're not, save the dessert for another time. If you are hungry, the best choices include fresh fruit, sorbet, frozen yogurt, sherbet or angel food cake with a fruit topping.
- Desserts aren't always off-limits, just keep your overall goals in mind. If you know ahead of time that you want dessert, plan to split your favorite treat with a companion. Another option is to eat slowly and to eat only a few bites.

More Survival Tips

- When eating out with family and friends, tell them in advance that you plan to eat healthy. Order what you know is best for you, and don't allow yourself to be tempted by others.

- If you know a meal will be high in calories and fat, choose more healthy foods during the rest of the day. Don't skip any meals!
- When eating at a buffet, plan in advance to choose healthier foods. Fill up on low-fat items such as fruits, vegetables, low-fat breads and crackers, and lean meats.
- When eating out, you can burn off a few extra calories by parking your car a few blocks away and walking. Make a plan to go for a walk before or after eating.

In the following table, list the restaurants where you dine most often. Next, list the foods that you usually order. Which foods would be better choices?

Restaurant	Usual Choices (be specific)	Better Choices

Reward yourself when you make good choices!

➤ What three things can you do to make healthier choices?

1.

2.

3.

CHANGING RECIPES

Low-fat cookbooks fill bookstore and library shelves. Perhaps you even have a collection of favorite cookbooks. If you like to cook and learn new recipes, that's great. But for most of us, learning all new recipes is not realistic. You don't have to buy a new cookbook or learn all new recipes to eat healthy and lose weight. You can make almost any recipe healthier with a few simple changes. Use the following tips to help turn your recipes into healthier alternatives.

JUST FOR STARTERS

- Which ingredients can be changed? Start by looking at ways to cut calories, fat, sugar and sodium.
- Find ways to increase nutrition by adding or substituting more healthful foods, such as whole grains, vegetables, legumes and fruits for less healthful foods, such as high-fat meats and refined grains.
- Make changes gradually to learn what works best. Changing ingredients can affect taste, texture and appearance.
- For that special occasion, don't change your favorite recipe—serve smaller portions.

CUT THE FAT

- Instead of frying meat, poultry and fish, broil, grill, roast or bake them. Use a rack or pans designed to catch drippings so that your meat won't cook in its own fat. Use lean meats trimmed of visible fat and skin.
- Use vegetable-oil spray and nonstick pots and pans instead of oils and butter for cooking.
- Baste, broil and stir-fry using small amounts of oil, broth, water or fruit juice.
- Limit meat portions in your recipes to three ounces or less per serving. Make up for the reduced meat by adding more grains, rice, pasta, vegetables or legumes.
- Use meat alternatives—beans, lentils, peas and soy products—in recipes calling for meat.
- Drain fat from meat during or after cooking. Rinse cooked ground meat with hot water to remove much of the fat.
- Refrigerate soups and stews before serving. Remove the layer of fat that hardens after cooling.
- In recipes calling for eggs, use cholesterol-free egg substitutes or substitute two egg whites for every whole egg.
- To cut the fat called for in a recipe by one-third to one-half, use vegetable oils instead of butter or shortening, and use low-fat or fat-free dairy products.
- In recipes calling for cheese, use one-third to one-half of what the recipe calls for. Use low-fat cheese with 3 to 5 grams of fat per 1-ounce serving.
- Use nonfat sour cream or make your own by mixing ½ cup of low-fat yogurt and ½ cup low-fat cottage cheese. Flavor with lemon juice and your favorite herbs and spices.

- Replace some of the fat in baked goods with fruit purees, such as prune, applesauce or banana, or nonfat dairy products such as nonfat yogurt. Use ½ cup of pureed fruit in place of 1 cup of butter, shortening or oil. Don't get rid of all the fat. You may need to add 1 to 2 tablespoons of fat back into the recipe to achieve the best results.
- Use low-fat or nonfat cream cheese, sour cream, yogurt, mayonnaise and salad dressing instead of the full-fat versions.

CUT THE SUGAR

- Try using one-third less sugar than what the recipe calls for.
- Substitute artificial sweeteners when appropriate. This will not work in many baked goods. Aspartame (NutraSweet, Equal) cannot be used in cooking—it loses its sweetness when heated. Splenda, however, can be used in cooking and baking.
- Learn to make special treats with fruits, such as fruit and yogurt smoothies, fruit pops, frozen bananas and trail mix.
- Experiment using fruit juice concentrates instead of sugar. You'll need to reduce the amount of overall liquid ingredients.
- Serve smaller portions of your favorite recipes.

CUT THE SODIUM

- Add flavor to vegetables, meats, poultry and fish with herbs and spices instead of using salt or high-sodium seasonings or sauces.
- Choose low-sodium versions of soups, broths and sauces.
- Eliminate or cut the salt in half for most of your recipes. Many seasoning packets in easy-to-fix meals (i.e., macaroni and cheese) are high in sodium. Use one-half or less of the packet or substitute your own seasonings.
- Rinse canned vegetables with water to wash away extra sodium.

ADD FIBER, VITAMINS AND MINERALS

- Increase fiber by substituting whole-wheat flour, oats or cornmeal for some of the flour in recipes. Substitute one-half of white flour in a recipe with whole-wheat flour, or substitute one-third of white flour with oats.
- Add puréed fruits or vegetables in place of some of the water in recipes.
- Keep the peels on fruits and vegetables such as potatoes, carrots and apples.
- Add extra vegetables or grains such as rice, pasta or legumes to soups, sauces, salads and casseroles.
- Top a baked potato with steamed, fresh or stir-fried vegetables.

MAKE SOME CHANGES

After reviewing the above suggestions, choose a few recipes to which you're willing to make changes. List them below.

Recipe/Food	Preparation/Ingredients	HealthyChange

MEATLESS MEALS

For many people, meat is part of their daily meal plan. Unfortunately, meat is at the top of the list of foods that contribute the most calories, fat, saturated fat and cholesterol to the American diet. You don't have to eat meat every day to meet your body's nutritional needs. Research shows that an eating plan high in fruits, vegetables, whole-grains and low-fat dairy products reduces the risk for many diseases, such as coronary heart disease, high blood pressure, diabetes and some forms of cancer. While we're not recommending you eat only vegetables and water, eating a few meatless meals may be a healthy addition to your eating plan.

REDUCING MEAT IN YOUR EATING PLAN

Following your Live-It plan will give your body the protein it needs. However, most Americans eat much more protein than they need for good health. Keep in mind what counts as a serving. Three ounces of meat is equal to a couple of sandwich slices of deli-style meat. Think about the size of a deck of playing cards or an audiocassette. What about typical portion sizes served in most restaurants? What portion sizes do you eat at home? As you can see, it's easy to eat more meat than you need.

One smart way to reduce your meat intake—and the fat and cholesterol that come with it—is to choose small portions of lean meats. Another way is to substitute other good sources of protein for meals that usually contain meat. Plant proteins can meet your body's daily needs, as long as you choose from a wide variety of protein-rich plant foods, such as whole grains, legumes, vegetables, low-fat dairy products, seeds and nuts. Remember, however, that some meatless sources of protein, such as cheese, nuts and seeds, can be high in calories and fat. In fact, cheese can be higher in fat and cholesterol than many meats. A good rule of thumb is the whiter the cheese, the lower the fat. However, a low-sodium cheese will be higher in fat than one with higher sodium.

The legume family—beans, peas, lentils and soybeans—provides a good source of protein. Legumes are also good sources of carbohydrates, B vitamins and many other essential vitamins and minerals. They're a great source of soluble fiber, which helps lower blood cholesterol levels. Soy products, such as tofu, are especially good substitutes for animal proteins. Use legumes as the main part of any meal or add them to dishes such as soups, sauces and casseroles that typically call for meat. Choose any variety you like: kidney beans, navy beans, black beans, peas and lentils—and in any form: dried, canned, fresh or frozen.

WHAT TO EAT INSTEAD OF MEAT

To help get you started, here are some suggestions for meatless meals:

- Vegetarian pizza: Instead of meats, pile on the vegetables.
- Spaghetti with meatless sauce: Add beans or other vegetables to the sauce instead of meat.

- Casseroles: Use beans, whole grains or extra vegetables for some or all of the meat in the recipe.
- Bean burrito: Watch out for beans refried in lard, and go easy on the cheese.
- Vegetarian soups: Replace the meat in soups with beans or whole grains, such as rice or pasta.
- Salads: Use beans, such as kidney or garbanzo, or low-fat cottage cheese instead of meat toppings.

MEATLESS MEALS AT HOME OR WHEN DINING OUT

Try some of these helpful ideas for meatless meals, or come up with your own.

Breakfast
- Whole-grain, ready-to-eat cereal and nonfat milk.
- Whole-grain toast, English muffin, bagel or toaster waffle with jam or jelly. You can add nonfat cream cheese or a little peanut butter as a source of protein.
- Low-fat yogurt is a great source of protein, calcium and other nutrients.

Lunch or Dinner
- Fresh vegetable salad, but go easy on the cheese. Add beans, peas, other legumes, nuts and seeds to boost protein, vitamins and minerals.
- Meatless soups, but choose broth-based instead of cream-based soups. Rice, pasta and other grains such as barley or tabouli are good substitutes for meat in many soups.
- Vegetable sandwich, but watch out for cheese and high-fat spreads such as cream cheese or mayonnaise. Try a vegetarian burger for a change of pace. These are usually made with whole grains, soy protein and other vegetables. They're lower in calories, fat and cholesterol than the traditional burger. Experiment until you find one you like.
- Prepare stir-fry with legumes, tofu or extra vegetables instead of meat.

Other Tips for Meatless Meals
- Choose restaurants with vegetarian dishes; many ethnic cuisines offer meatless dishes.
- Order salads, soups, breads and fruits if a restaurant doesn't offer meatless dishes.
- When traveling, call the airline at least 48 hours in advance to request a meatless meal.

Beside meat, what's another food that provides the most calories, fat, saturated fat and cholesterol in the American diet? Cheese! It's common for people who are trying to eat less meat to substitute cheese instead. Watch out! Ounce for ounce, regular cheese has more fat and saturated fat than many cuts of meat. Be sure to choose reduced-fat cheeses as often as possible. Choose cheeses with 3 to 5 grams of fat per ounce.

MAKE SOME CHANGES

Are you ready to add a few meatless meals to your eating plan? Using the above tips or some ideas of your own, list a few ideas you're ready to try:

Food/Meal	Changes I Will Make

CALCULATING EXCHANGES FOR A RECIPE

1. List each ingredient and the amount that the recipe calls for.
2. Exchange each ingredient by using the Live-It plan or another book that lists the exchanges per food item.
3. Add up the total in each exchange column.
4. Divide each exchange total by the number of servings.

Note: You must know (or estimate) how many servings are in the recipe. Some exchange columns will need to be rounded off to the nearest 1/2 exchange.

SAMPLE RECIPE CONVERSION CHART

Recipe: _Mexican Layer Dip_   **Number of Servings:** 24   **Serving Size:** _1/24 of pan_

Exchange per Serving: _1/2 meat, 1/2 fat, 16 calories_

Ingredients	Amounts	Exchanges						
		Bread	Meat	Veggies	Fruit	Milk	Fat	Free
Fat-Free Refried Beans	16 ounces	4	2					
Avocado	medium						8	
Lemon Juice	1 tablespoon							*
Fat-Free Sour Cream	16 ounces							
Taco Seasoning	1 package							*
Fat-Free Cheddar Cheese	12 ounces		12					
Green Chilies	4.5 ounces			2				
Tomatoes	2 medium			2				
Black Olives	4.25 ounces						4	
Total Each Exchange		4	14	4	*	*	12	*
Divide by Number Servings		24	24	24	24	24	24	24
Exchanges per Serving		*	1/2	*	*	*	1/2	*

* This amount is less than 1/4 of an exchange

RECIPE CONVERSION CHART

Recipe: _____ Number of Servings: _____ Serving Size: _____

Exchange per Serving: _____

Ingredients	Amounts	Exchanges						
		Bread	Meat	Veggies	Fruit	Milk	Fat	Free
Total Each Exchange								
Divide by Number Servings								
Exchanges per Serving								

PREVENTING OSTEOPOROSIS

Osteoporosis is one of the most significant health problems in this country. Over 25 million Americans, mostly postmenopausal women, are affected by osteoporosis—but men are affected too! Osteoporosis results in over 1.5 million fractures each year. Unfortunately, in the elderly many of these fractures result in significant disability—even death! The seriousness of osteoporosis makes low calcium intake one of the most important nutrition-related problems in the country. Only 20 percent of women meet the daily recommended intake for calcium. A sedentary lifestyle is also a major risk factor.

WHAT IS OSTEOPOROSIS?

Osteoporosis is a weakening of the bones that results from the gradual loss of calcium and other minerals. These weak bones can easily fracture during a fall. They can even break during normal activities! The spine, hip and wrist are the most common sites for fracture. Unfortunately, this disease is often silent and the first symptoms are fracture and disability.

Fortunately, osteoporosis can be prevented—and treated. Prevention is best begun in childhood because the amount of bone—what doctors call peak bone mass—achieved before the age of 35 is an important predictor of risk. The key to prevention is building healthy bones through good nutrition, regular physical activity, a healthy lifestyle and medical therapy when appropriate—it's never too late to start!

UNDERSTANDING RISK FACTORS

Check off risk factors that may affect you.

- ☐ Caucasian and Asian woman are at a higher risk.
- ☐ Your risk is higher if you're underweight or small boned.
- ☐ Osteoporosis runs in families. What's your family history?
- ☐ The rate of bone loss increases rapidly after menopause, whether natural or surgical. The body's estrogen helps women maintain and build healthy bones. Are you postmenopausal?

Tips

- Hormone replacement therapy can slow bone loss after menopause. Talk to your doctor to see if hormones are right for you.
- Regular weight-bearing physical activity throughout life builds healthy bones. How active are you?
- Smoking promotes bone loss. If you smoke, quit!
- Calcium and other vitamins and minerals are essential for good bone health. How's your calcium intake?

- Diets high in protein, sodium and caffeine have little effect on bone health. Unfortunately, soft drinks, tea and coffee often replace good sources of calcium, such as nonfat milk and fortified orange juice.
- Eating disorders such as bulimia and anorexia nervosa are associated with poor bone health and osteoporosis.

UNDERSTANDING CALCIUM

Calcium is essential for bone health, but it also has several other important roles in the body such as nerve function, muscle contraction and blood clotting. The body contains more calcium than any other mineral. Most of your calcium—99 percent—is stored in your bones. If you don't get enough calcium from your diet, your body steals it from your bones. Milk, yogurt and cheese supply 75 percent of dietary calcium. A high intake of dietary calcium may also prevent high blood pressure and colon cancer.

ARE YOU GETTING ENOUGH?

Although it's easy to get all the calcium you need from a healthy eating plan, the majority of women only get about half of the calcium they need for bone health. Most adults should get around 1,200 milligrams of calcium each day. If your risk for osteoporosis is high, some experts recommend 1,500 milligrams. Check out this high-calcium eating plan:

Three servings of low-fat dairy (a serving is 8 ounces of milk or yogurt)	~ 900 to 1000 mg
1 to 1.5 oz. of cheese (a single sandwich slice or a cube the size of your thumb)	~ 200 mg
8 ounces of calcium-fortified orange juice	~ 300 mg
Healthful diet (dark green leafy vegetables, fruits, whole grains and legumes)	~ 200 to 400 mg
Total	~ 1600 to 1900 mg

If you're lactose intolerant or a strict vegetarian (no dairy), it can be more difficult to meet your daily calcium needs. Many people who are lactose intolerant can drink smaller servings of milk—start with 2-to-4 ounce servings—or drink it with meals. Yogurt, cheese and buttermilk are often easier to digest. Try using a reduced lactose milk or lactase enzyme. Other good sources of calcium include tofu processed with calcium and calcium-fortified foods such as orange juice, soy milk and cereals. Make sure to eat lots of dark green leafy vegetables, fruits, whole grains, legumes and nuts, too.

WHAT ABOUT CALCIUM SUPPLEMENTS?

Food sources are your first choice because they contain other important nutrients your body needs. However, if your diet falls short, a supplement may be a good idea. Talk to your doctor about what's best for you. If you choose to supplement, only supplement the amount of calcium you need—small doses of 250 to 500 milligrams are best. It's best to take a calcium supplement with a meal to help absorption. Calcium carbonate and calcium citrate are good sources. Daily intake of calcium greater than 2,500 milligrams increase the risk of kidney stones.

WHAT ABOUT PHYSICAL ACTIVITY?

Studies show that active men and women have healthier bones. The bones adapt to the stress of regular weight-bearing physical activity by becoming stronger. Good activities include walking, jogging, aerobics, strength training and recreational sports that keep you on your feet. Recent studies show that strength training can slow down and even reverse the loss of bone that occurs in postmenopausal women. Doing some activity in the sunshine a few days a week can give you an additional boost—more vitamin D!

A WORD ABOUT VITAMIN D

Vitamin D is also important—it helps your body use calcium to build healthy bones. If you drink milk, you're likely getting enough vitamin D. Your skin can also produce vitamin D with the help of sunshine; 10 to 15 minutes a few days each week is all you need. If you don't drink milk or you get little sunshine, you may need to consider a supplement.

THE TRUTH ABOUT FATS

"Low fat," "fat free," "nonfat," "no fat," "less fat," "reduced fat"—too much fat! Surveys reveal that dietary fat is the number one nutritional concern of Americans. In fact, reducing dietary fat has become an obsession for many. Despite our knowledge about fat and the availability of more low-fat foods, the number of Americans who are overweight or obese is on the rise.

FATS ARE ESSENTIAL FOR GOOD HEALTH!

Fats are an important source of energy. They supply, carry and store the fat-soluble vitamins—A, D, E and K. Fats are involved in the production of nerve cells, cell membranes and many important hormones. Fat helps your body maintain healthy skin and hair. Body fat cushions and insulates the body. Fat also gives certain foods their taste, texture and aroma. Fat satisfies hunger and makes many foods more pleasurable to eat. However, too much fat in the diet is associated with heart disease, certain cancers, diabetes, obesity and high blood pressure.

HOW MUCH FAT DO I NEED?

With about 34 percent of calories, the typical American diet is still too high in fat. The goal is to keep total fat intake to 30 percent of calories or less. Fat contains nine calories per gram, which is over twice the calories supplied by carbohydrates and proteins. Because high-fat foods contain more calories, they probably increase the likelihood of weight gain. However, too many calories and not enough physical activity are the real problems. Even eating low-fat foods high in calories will result in weight gain.

Variety, balance and moderation are the keys to a healthy eating plan. Cutting fat without cutting calories or without getting more physical activity will not help you lose weight. The Live-It plan provides a healthy balance of fat that makes up between 20 to 30 percent of total calories.

DIFFERENT TYPES OF FAT

All fats are made up of carbon, hydrogen and oxygen molecules and are classified by their chemical structure—saturated, polyunsaturated and monounsaturated. Most foods contain all three types of fats but in different amounts.

Saturated
- "Saturated" refers to a fat that has all the hydrogen molecules it can hold. This saturation with hydrogen creates a rigid structure that is solid at room temperature.
- Saturated fats raise blood cholesterol levels more than any other type of fat. Animal foods such as meat, poultry, fish, butter, milk and cheese are high in saturated fats. Coconut oil, palm oil and palm kernel oil are also high in saturated fat.

Polyunsaturated and Monounsaturated

- Polyunsaturated and monounsaturated fats are not saturated with hydrogen molecules. Because they are unsaturated, they have flexible structures that are fluid at room temperature. Vegetable oils are higher in unsaturated fats.
- Polyunsaturated fats may help decrease blood cholesterol levels when substituted for saturated fats. Common sources of polyunsaturated fats are safflower oil, sunflower oil, corn oil, soybean oil and many nuts and seeds.
- Monounsaturated fats also help decrease blood cholesterol levels when substituted for saturated fats. Common sources of monounsaturated fats are olive oil, canola oil, peanut oil and avocados.

CUTTING DOWN FAT

When it comes to calories, all fats are created equal. Because all fats are high in calories, cutting back on fat can help you consume fewer calories and lose weight—physical activity helps too! The highest sources of dietary fat are found in meats, cheese, eggs, dairy products, desserts, snack foods and nuts. The key to low-fat eating is learning to choose the foods highest in nutrition and lowest in calories—whole grains, fruits, vegetables, lean meats, poultry, fish and low-fat dairy products. Much of the fat in our diet is added—butter, margarine, cheese, oils and salad dressings. Use less of these fats in cooking and preparation. Also, make the switch to low-fat or nonfat alternatives when available. But remember, not all low-fat versions of cakes, cookies or snack foods are low calorie!

Here are some more helpful tips for cutting down on the fat and saturated fat in your eating plan.

Eat Less Saturated Fat

Saturated fat is the main culprit when it comes to high blood cholesterol levels. Specifically, eating lots of saturated fat will increase the LDL cholesterol, which is the bad cholesterol that's linked to fatty buildup in the arteries. Certain cancers may also be related to higher intakes of saturated fat. That's why it's especially important to limit intake of this type of fat.

Meat is where Americans get most of the saturated fat and cholesterol in their diet—although cheese is a close second. Instead of fatty meats, look for lean cuts of beef and pork, usually labeled "loin" or "round." And look for lean or extra lean ground beef, chicken or turkey. Buy cuts labeled "select" rather than "prime" or "choice." Remove extra fat and use low-fat cooking methods—grill, boil, broil, bake and roast instead of frying. Look for reduced-fat or fat-free versions of luncheon meats and hot dogs.

More Helpful Tips

- Use all fats and oils sparingly, selecting polyunsaturated and monounsaturated fats instead of saturated fats such as butter, lard, shortening and tropical oils (coconut, palm and palm kernel).
- Drink nonfat or low-fat milk (1%) and choose low-fat or nonfat versions of yogurt and sour cream.
- Learn to modify your recipes with low-fat substitutions.

- Limit the amount of cheese in your eating plan. Choose cheeses with three to five grams of fat per ounce. Use ⅓ to ½ less cheese than a recipe calls for. You can even mix low-fat and nonfat versions to cut down on fat and calories. Ounce for ounce, cheese is as high in saturated fat as meat!
- Choose low-fat salad dressings and mayonnaise with no more than 1 gram of saturated fat per tablespoon. Choose mustard, ketchup and other low-fat spreads and condiments more often.
- Limit the number of eggs you eat each week to two or three. Or substitute two egg whites for every whole egg—the yolks contain most of the fat and cholesterol—or use cholesterol-free egg substitutes.
- Use low-fat cooking methods. Make low-fat substitutions in your recipes; sauté using low-sodium broth instead of oils and other fats; chill soups and stews and skim off the fat that collects on the surface.
- Cut down on bakery and snack foods—cakes, cookies, pastries, doughnuts and chips. Even low-fat versions can be high in calories!

Note: Children below the age of two should not follow a fat-restricted diet.

CHOOSING HIGH-FIBER FOODS

Many of the foods you eat influence your risk for several diseases, including heart disease, stroke, diabetes and certain cancers. Following an eating plan that is high in fiber and low in saturated fat and cholesterol reduces your risk for these diseases. High-fiber foods may also help you achieve and maintain a healthy weight. Health experts recommend that you eat 25 to 30 grams of fiber each day; the national average is 15 grams or less!

You can get all the fiber you need if you eat a variety of foods, including:

- Six to eleven servings of bread, cereal, rice, pasta and other grains daily. At least three servings from this group should include whole-grain foods.
- Five or more servings of fruits and vegetables daily.
- Legumes—beans, peas, soybeans and lentils—at least once or twice each week.

WHAT FIBER IS

Fiber is found only in the cell walls of plants—fruits, vegetables and grains. Your body does not digest or absorb fiber. Grains are made up of three parts—bran, endosperm and germ. Most processed grain foods are made from the endosperm. The endosperm contains the energy—carbohydrates and protein—but little of the fiber, vitamins, minerals and phytochemicals (plant chemicals believed to promote health). Whole grains also contain the bran and the germ, which are higher in fiber and nutrients. There are two main types of fiber in the diet—soluble and insoluble.

Soluble fiber dissolves in water and forms a gel in the digestive system. The texture of foods like cooked oatmeal comes from soluble fiber. Soluble fiber lowers blood cholesterol levels by blocking the absorption of cholesterol and fats from the diet. It may also have other cholesterol-lowering effects. In fact, scientists have isolated a component of soluble fiber called beta-glucan that appears to be responsible for many of these benefits. Soluble fiber may also help lower blood sugar. Good sources of soluble fiber include oatmeal, oat bran, barley, dried beans, peas, brown rice and apples.

Insoluble fiber does not dissolve in water. Insoluble fiber is more important in digestive health. It provides the roughage that improves bowel function and lowers your risk of colon cancer. Except for being a substitute for foods higher in fat and cholesterol, insoluble fiber does not appear to lower cholesterol levels. Good sources of insoluble fiber are whole-grain breads and cereals, wheat bran and most fruits and vegetables.

DIETARY FIBER AND WEIGHT CONTROL

Both types of fiber may help in weight control. High-fiber foods are more filling and less fattening (i.e., they are usually lower in calories and fat). Also, eating meals that are high in fiber—fruits, vegetables, whole grains and legumes—leaves less room for foods that are high in calories and fat. Very high fiber, low-calorie diets are not good ways to lose weight because they come up short in other important nutrients. Fiber supplements are also not recommended for weight loss. Balance, moderation and variety are the keys to good nutrition!

GETTING ENOUGH OF THE RIGHT KIND OF FIBER

Do you eat three servings of whole grains each day? Experts recommend that at least 3 of the 6 to 11 servings of breads, cereals, rice and pasta that you eat every day be whole grains. White and wheat breads, white rice, refined pasta and many cereals do not count as whole grain. Look for whole grain, multigrain or whole wheat on the label. Don't let the names "wheat bread" and "wheat cereal" fool you—these foods are often colored with caramel or molasses. Look at the label—does it contain 2 or more grams of fiber per serving?

What foods can you add to your eating plan to boost your intake of fiber? Sticking with the Live-It plan will give you at least five servings of fruits and vegetables and six servings of breads, cereals, rice, pasta and other grains each day. This should give you most of the fiber you need each day. For extra insurance, make sure that you're choosing several foods that are high in fiber. Review the following table.

➤ Do you eat at least five grams of soluble fiber every day? What foods do you regularly eat that are high in soluble fiber?

Food	Serving	Fiber (in grams)	Soluble	Insoluble
White bread	1 slice	Less than 1		
Wheat bread	1 slice	Less than 1		
White rice	1/2 cup	Less than 1		
Refined pasta	1/2 cup	Less than 1		
Graham crackers	2 squares	2		✓
Broccoli	1/2 cup	2		✓
Orange	1 medium	2		✓
Whole-wheat bread	1 slice	2 to 3		✓
Whole-grain bread	1 slice	2 to 3		✓
Whole-wheat pasta	1/2 cup	2 to 3		✓
Bran muffin	1 medium	2 to 3	✓	✓
Oats, oatmeal	3/4 cup	3	✓	✓
Apple with skin	1 medium	3	✓	✓
Brown rice	1/2 cup	3 to 4	✓	✓
Potato with skin	1 medium	3 to 4	✓	✓
Legumes and peas	1/2 cup	4 to 6	✓	✓
Bran cereal	1/2 cup	6 to 15	✓	✓

INCREASING THE FIBER IN YOUR DIET

- Choose more whole- or multigrain breads. Look for whole-wheat or whole-grain flour as the first ingredient.
- Start your day with a bowl of whole-grain or bran cereal.
- Try adding $\frac{1}{4}$ cup of wheat bran to foods such as cereal, pancakes, applesauce, yogurt or meat loaf.
- When baking, substitute whole-wheat flour for half of the white flour called for in the recipe.
- In baked goods, substitute oats for one-third of the flour called for in the recipe.
- Mix at least one-half refined pasta or white rice with whole-grain pasta or brown rice in dishes.
- Increase your intake of beans, lentils, soybeans and peas. Use instead of meat in casseroles or other dishes.
- Add legumes, wheat bran or other grains to soups, pasta, salads and other dishes.
- Leave the skin on fruits and vegetables such as apples, pears, peaches and potatoes.
- Add fresh or dried fruits to cereals and salads.
- Add extra vegetables to salads, soups and other dishes.
- Read food labels. Foods with more than 2.5 grams of fiber per serving are good sources of fiber.

OFF TO A GOOD START

Breakfast may be the most important meal of the day. After all, your body hasn't had any food for 8 to 12 hours—it's time to break the fast. After a night's sleep, your body needs a fresh supply of fuel and nutrients to start the day. Your mind needs energy to be sharp. Your muscles need energy to keep you on the move. A healthy breakfast gives your body what it needs.

RESEARCH RESULTS

- Several studies show that breakfast eaters perform better mentally and physically.
- Some studies suggest that breakfast skippers are more likely to overeat later in the day. Approaching snack time or lunch on an empty stomach can lead to poor choices and overeating.
- Studies show that regular breakfast eaters consume more nutrients throughout the day. Regular breakfast eaters are more likely to get adequate levels of minerals, such as calcium, phosphorus and magnesium and vitamins, such as riboflavin, folate and vitamins A, C and B_{12}.
- One study of nearly 3,500 men and women found that regular cereal eaters eat less fat during the day, have a lower cholesterol intake and eat more fiber. They also have lower blood cholesterol levels. All these factors add up to a lower risk for heart disease.

➥ Unfortunately, despite all the benefits of starting the day with a healthy breakfast, it's the meal most often skipped. Do you skip breakfast? What are your reasons?

☐ I'm not hungry in the morning.   ☐ I don't need the calories.
☐ I don't have enough time.   ☐ Other_____
☐ I don't enjoy eating breakfast.   ☐ Other_____

➥ If you do eat breakfast, are you making healthy choices? Make a list of your typical breakfast foods. How do they stack up nutritionally?

STARTING THE DAY NUTRITIONALLY RIGHT

While eating any kind of breakfast may be better than skipping, it's important to make healthy choices. Soft drinks, sugary cereals, pastries, fried potatoes and high-fat meats are not a healthy way to go. These foods supply calories your body needs for energy but can be high in fat, cholesterol and sugar and low in vitamins, minerals and fiber. A balanced breakfast will give you the sustained energy and nutrients your body needs.

Try to eat a well-balanced breakfast high in complex carbohydrates, some protein and a little fat. Whole-grain cereals and breads, nonfat milk, yogurt, fruit and even eggs are good choices. These foods stay with you longer and give you the energy you need to make it through the morning. Many breakfast foods are high in simple sugars and can quickly leave you feeling hungry again.

CEREAL—A GREAT START TO ANY DAY

Hot and cold cereals are a great start to any day. Fortified cereals provide vitamins, such as folate and other B vitamins, and minerals, such as iron and calcium. Adding low-fat or nonfat milk boosts the protein, B vitamins and minerals such as calcium, phosphorus and magnesium. High-fiber cereals help keep your digestive system working regularly and provide other important health benefits. Balance out your breakfast and get a start on your five-a-day by eating fresh fruit with your cereal.

Read the Nutrition Facts label and the ingredient list to find the cereals best for you. Look for high-fiber, low-sugar and vitamin-fortified brands. You want the first ingredients listed to be whole grains or rolled oats. Look for cereals with 5 to 10 grams of sugar or less and greater than 2.5 grams of fiber per serving. Low-fat cereals have no more than 2 to 3 grams of fat—watch out for granola, which is often high in fat and sugar. Some varieties of cereal are fortified with 100 percent of the recommended daily allowance for vitamins and minerals—just make sure to finish the milk in the bottom of the bowl!

GETTING CREATIVE

What are some creative and enjoyable ways you can begin to make a healthy breakfast part of your daily routine? Try these tips to help get you started:

- Make sure you wake up in time to fit in a good breakfast—10 to 15 minutes is all you need. To save time, prepare for breakfast before you go to bed.
- If you don't have time to eat at home or if you're not hungry first thing in the morning, drink a small glass of low-fat or nonfat milk, or fruit or vegetable juice on the way to work. You can pack a bagel, breakfast bar, yogurt, peanut-butter sandwich, cheese and crackers or fresh fruit to eat on the way to or at work.
- Make eating breakfast a family affair. Start the day connecting with your family and fueling your bodies for the day ahead. What a great opportunity to start the day with prayer!
- It takes just minutes to make a delicious smoothie. Simply mix nonfat yogurt, frozen fruit and juice or milk in a blender—experiment! Drink it while you're getting ready or on your way to work.
- Pop frozen waffles (preferably whole grain) into the toaster and top with jam, jelly, yogurt, low-fat cream cheese or peanut butter. You can do the same with whole-grain breads, bagels or English muffins.
- Skip the fat-laden breakfast sandwiches offered by fast-food chains. Make your own from low-fat cheese, lean ham or turkey, bread, bagel or an English muffin.

- Who says you have to eat a traditional breakfast in the morning? Leftover vegetable pizza, grilled cheese sandwiches, burritos and other lunch and dinnertime favorites are options you can choose. You can have a quick and nutritious breakfast by reheating leftovers.

Try to come up with your own creative ideas. What are some things you can do to make breakfast a healthy start to your day?

BREAKFAST IN THE FAST LANE

Do you find yourself eating breakfast away from home or in the car? Are you able to make healthy choices?

- Hot and cold cereals are a good choice at any restaurant.
- Pancakes and waffles can be a good choice if you go easy on the butter or margarine. Top them with fresh fruit, jam, jelly or syrup.
- Order fruit juice and low-fat milk instead of coffee or a soft drink for breakfast.
- Eggs are a good choice because they are a good source of protein, iron and vitamin A. It's the egg yolks that are high in cholesterol; ask for scrambled eggs made without the yolk or with an egg substitute.
- A bagel or English muffin is a good choice, but watch the butter and cream cheese. Most muffins are high in fat and calories, as are pastries, croissants and biscuits.

Maintenance

MAINTAINING YOUR HEALTHY WEIGHT
STAYING THE COURSE

Congratulations! You've reached your weight goal! And what's more, you've established a new, healthier lifestyle. Because of your choices, you've become a new person. But remember, the reading on the scale is not the reward. Having an enjoyable, energetic and effective life is the reward!

IT'S A JOURNEY, NOT A DESTINATION

Of course, reaching that weight goal is not your final destination either. It's just a marker event on the journey. Now it's time to think about the long-term challenges ahead: keeping the weight off, living out those healthy choices one day at a time, learning from your mistakes, putting the Lord in first place, trusting His plans and responding to daily challenges by looking to Him for every need.

However, maintaining a right perspective toward food and body image isn't easy in our beauty-conscious, high-tech, instant-gratification society in which discipline and endurance are not highly prized. Yet these are the very character traits you'll need in order to stick to that healthy lifestyle and weight.

For that reason this maintenance program is designed to help you continue developing those traits. It includes reminders, encouraging Scripture verses and practical tools to help you set reasonable goals, pace yourself for the long run, measure your successes by God's standards and stay the course.

HOW TO USE THIS MAINTENANCE SECTION

This maintenance section has been divided into eight segments that can easily be completed in eight weeks as you make the transition from losing weight to maintaining the weight you have lost. Each week's session includes an article to help you focus on the topic, Stepping Stones to help you focus on the key principles, Stepping Back to give you an opportunity to reflect on what has been learned and Stepping Forward to help you apply what you have learned to your present walk with Christ.

Let us not become weary in doing good, for at the proper time we will reap a harvest if we do not give up (Galatians 6:9).

CONGRATULATIONS!
YOU HAVE REACHED YOUR LIFETIME GOAL!

 When you have reached your *lifetime* weight loss goal *and* maintained it for eight weeks, *First Place* will recognize your accomplishments by sending you a special gift after we receive this completed form. The form must be signed by your *First Place* leader.

AT-GOAL FORM

Today's Date _____ Date of Birth _____

Name _____

Street Address _____

City, State, Zip Code _____

Home Phone _____ E-mail _____

First Place Location _____

Current Leader(s) _____

Street Address _____

City, State, Zip Code _____

Beginning Date_____ Beginning Weight _____

Goal Date_____ Goal Weight _____

My life before coming to First Place:

The circumstances that led me to join First Place:

The truth I have come to understand in First Place:

The effects of First Place on my life:

- Physical

- Mental

- Emotional

- Spiritual

A word of encouragement to others about my experience:

If available, please include photos of yourself before and after your weight loss.

Please sign below if you will give First Place permission to use this information in a future First Place publication or website.

Signature	Date

Leader's Signature	Date

Please mail this form to:
First Place
7401 Katy Freeway
Houston, TX 77024

RUNNING TO WIN

THE SECRETS OF SUCCESSFUL MAINTAINERS

Live by Principle

It's really no secret. People who successfully keep off extra weight all follow the same basic First Place guidelines. First, they live by principle rather than impulse. They continually look to God for grace to make good long-term choices, rather than choosing what feels good momentarily. They orient life around loving God and others, not around self—keeping their eyes on Him and off the refrigerator or scale. Their motives are solid and enduring, not fickle and fleeting.

Know the Facts

Successful maintainers remember the facts about weight and metabolic balance. They're determined to enjoy healthy food choices: fresh fruits, vegetables, whole grains, lean meats. Not dwelling on what they can't eat, they gratefully accept God's bountiful provision of healthy options. Plus, they've built healthy habits—eating only when hungry, controlling portions and stopping when full.

Stay Physically Active

Successful maintainers stay active. They've made at least one enjoyable exercise a priority several times a week. In fact, 90 percent of successful maintainers follow a healthy eating plan *and* a regular physical-activity program. They strive to build muscle and declare war on slothfulness. They find ways throughout the day to exert their bodies, boosting their energy level and zest for living: walking or biking instead of driving, taking the stairs, playing outside with the kids or doing yard work or housework with a vengeance. They choose service over entertainment.

Have Goals and Support

Maintainers also have written realistic goals, a plan for reaching them and like-minded support. Their objectives are not superficial ones, such as a dress size or a perfect body, but healthy lifestyle goals. They've accepted their God-given physical stature, not comparing themselves with others. Their goals are clear and attainable. They monitor their progress with the encouragement and help of a few accountability partners. They know their weaknesses and have a plan to counter them.

Keep on Going

Most importantly, maintainers don't give up. Clear priorities help them keep first things first so that a slipup isn't a failure and a major life change doesn't cause them to jump ship. Successful maintainers simply regroup, learn and move on—one day at a time. You see, they're not on a diet, and their rules are not rigid. Instead, healthy eating and activity have become a lifestyle, not an event.

Run in such a way that you will win (1 Corinthians 9:24, *NLT*).

STEPPING STONES

- Live by principle, not by impulse.
- Have written, realistic goals.
- Remember the facts about weight and metabolic balance.
- Determine to enjoy healthy food choices.
- Remain active.
- Have a long-range plan for monitoring and reaching goals.
- Stick with your First Place group.
- Commit to keep on going, no matter what.
- Keep first things first.

STEPPING BACK

Pause, Study and Reflect

➣ What does it mean to you to live by principle rather than impulse?

➣ According to 1 Corinthians 9:24,25, what does Paul mean by running "in such a way that you will win" (*NLT*).

➣ Identify the theme of Colossians 1:9-18, explaining how it pertains to your new lifestyle. Memorize verses 10 through 12.

STEPPING FORWARD

Make It Work for You

➣ From the above Stepping Stones, write down those that are the most critical for the Lord to teach you right now.

REVIEWING HIS PROVISION

CONSIDER HOW FAR YOU'VE COME

Look Back
You can learn to live by the success principles just discussed and maintain your healthy weight, but you must start from where you are. Take a minute to consider how far you've come and review how God has brought you to this point.

Consider His Grace
God's Word explains that all good things come from His hand. If you've trusted Jesus Christ's work on the cross as payment for your sin, it is by God's grace that you've done so. In the same way, His grace enables believers to actually live lives that please Him.

It's entirely His grace that has allowed you to put Him in first place and to put eating in its proper place. So thankfully consider how He has helped you, reflecting on the benefits your new weight and healthy lifestyle have already brought. Also take time to remember the obstacles He's helped you overcome.

Consider Your Goals
Review your original weight-loss incentives, determining which are still pertinent and which need adjusting. To maintain your new healthy habits, you'll need solid, unchanging, meaningful motives: a desire to treat your body as a temple and a desire for abundant energy to serve God effectively.

However, motives such as pleasing others, gaining attention or fitting into a certain pair of jeans are too superficial to help in the long run. Worse yet, they may bring feelings of guilt, failure and disappointment rather than encouraging you to strive for success.

STEPPING STONES

- Reviewing God's provision prepares you to move forward.
- All good things come from His hand.
- Consider how He's already helped you reach your goals.
- Consider the obstacles He's helped you overcome.
- Ascertain that your motives are solid, lasting and meaningful so that you'll persevere in your new healthy habits.

STEPPING BACK

Pause, Study and Reflect
Thank the Lord for His help thus far, and commit to continual reliance on Him for grace to help in time of need.

➺ What attitude toward God do Psalm 16:2 and Proverbs 3:5,6 convey?

➺ Consider and list those Scripture verses God has used to encourage, correct and exhort you—toward good eating and exercise habits, healthy relationships, effective conflict/stress management, etc.

 Ask the Lord to help you live for Him, rather than for yourself.

STEPPING FORWARD

Make It Work for You

➺ List the benefits you've experienced in achieving your goal weight (for example, more energy, increased fitness, better health, time for relationships, less self-centeredness).

➺ Anticipate and list obstacles to long-term maintenance of your new healthy weight.

➺ Review your original reasons for losing weight. At this point, why do you want to maintain this new weight and lifestyle? Will these motives last?

Whatever we do, it is because Christ's love controls us. Since we believe that Christ died for everyone, we also believe that we have all died to the old life we used to live. He died for everyone so that those who receive his new life will no longer live to please themselves. Instead, they will live to please Christ, who died and was raised for them (2 Corinthians 5:14,15, NLT).

THE BALANCING ACT

THE FACTS ABOUT WEIGHT AND METABOLISM

Beware

Losing weight is easy compared to the challenge of keeping it off. Nearly 50 percent of those who've lost weight regain it within one year! And sadly enough, after five years, a whopping 95 percent have returned to their beginning weight.

Be Prepared

But don't let this discourage you! Let it encourage you to be diligent and realistic in developing an effective weight-maintenance plan. Make it fit your lifestyle. Make sure you can call it your own. And make sure it's based on the facts.

Be Balanced

First, recall that your body gains, maintains or loses weight based on an efficient internal balance mechanism—your metabolism. It speeds up or slows down according to the daily effort required to move your body around. It's fueled by the calories you take in. Given more fuel than it needs, it stores food as fat and you gain weight. Given less fuel than required, it burns existing body fat for energy, and you lose weight. The key to weight maintenance is always calorie balance, continuing to take in just the amount your body needs.

Be Committed

Your new, lighter body requires less fuel to move it around and fewer calories to stay in balance than it did before you lost weight. As a result, your metabolism may have slowed down some. These facts mean that you can't return to your old eating habits and maintain your new weight. You must stick with your new ways!

Be Busy

Regular physical exercise can speed up your metabolism and make up for any slowing that's occurred, allowing for a few extra calories over time without weight gain! So the most important lifestyle choice you can maintain—besides healthy eating habits—is to continue to be physically active. This means sticking with a vigorous physical exercise you enjoy and making it a priority several times a week. It also may mean weight lifting two to three times per week to increase your body's muscle-to-fat ratio, further speeding up your metabolism. And it definitely means choosing to be an active person. Keep fighting against those sedentary aspects of your life!

STEPPING STONES

- A well thought-out maintenance program is critical to keeping the weight off.
- Bodies gain, maintain or lose weight based on their metabolic balance—calories burned versus calories consumed
- You cannot return to your previous eating habits and still maintain your new healthy weight.
- Regular physical exercise can speed up your metabolism and keep you at a steady weight despite the slowing effects of weight loss.

STEPPING BACK

Pause, Study and Reflect

Successful weight maintenance is the result of an internal biological balance. Who designed this complex system? Read Psalm 139:13-18 and consider your Creator's trustworthiness. Then commit to relying on the effectiveness of His design, plan your habits accordingly and be prepared for the long run. There's no reason to take short cuts or abandon your plan.

STEPPING FORWARD

Make It Work for You

➤ Before you lost weight, what unhealthy eating habits did you follow that you might be tempted to return to?

➤ List tactics for overcoming those temptations. Pray about it right now.

In the Take Aim section (pp. 174-176), you'll work out your new maintenance goals in terms of calories and a Live-It plan.

Your Balancing Act

Finding Your New Basal Metabolic Rate

Use the formula appropriate for your gender, then fill in your new weight, height and age in the corresponding sections of the table. To calculate your new basal metabolic rate, add Column A to Column B, then subtract Column C.

	Column A	Column B	Column C	BMR
Formula for Men	66 + (6.2 x weight in pounds)	12.7 x height in inches	6.8 x age in years	(A + B) – C = BMR Expressed as required calories per day
Formula for Women	655 + (4.4 x weight in pounds)	4.3 x height in inches	4.7 x age in years	(A + B) – C = BMR
My Formula	____ + (____ x ____) = _____ **A**	____ x ____ = _____ **B**	____ x ____ = _____ **C**	(____ +____) –_____ A　　B　　C = _____ **Your BMR**

Next, determine how your planned level of physical activity will impact your BMR. If you stick with your physical-activity goals, this number will accurately represent your new metabolic rate, affecting your maintenance calorie needs computation in the Taking Aim section.

Resting BMR	Activity Factor	Metabolic Rate (adjusted for physical activity factor)
My BMR _____	1.2 for sedentary lifestyle 1.4 for moderately active lifestyle 1.6 for vigorously active lifestyle My activity factor = _____	My BMR_____ x activity factor_____ = My adjusted metabolic rate_____

STANDING ON FIRM GROUND

INCORPORATE HEALTHY NUTRITION AND ACTIVITY PRINCIPLES

Embrace Principles

As you look toward the future and plan for successful long-term weight maintenance, remember to incorporate the key principles from the First Place recommendations for nutritional health found in this *Member's Guide*. Commit these unchanging guidelines to memory; they'll help you continue to make good daily eating and exercise decisions, adapt well to unpredictable situations and be successful in the long run.

Eat for Overall Health

Maintain practical, enjoyable eating habits, focusing on nourishment, well-being and general health. Remember to eat slowly and choose small portions. Keep including a variety of foods: whole grains, fresh fruits and vegetables, lean meats, poultry, fish and low-fat dairy products. Avoid foods high in fat, cholesterol, sodium and sugar. Drink eight glasses of water per day to stay hydrated, burn fat and prevent water retention or bloating. Eat only until comfortably full.

Enjoy Activity

Stay active. Don't consider exercise as torturous work. Instead, make activity a lifelong mind-set—a regular part of your day. This perspective will help you enjoy life more and more as you feel increasingly fit. In fact, your growing fitness level will bring you pleasure not only during your exercise sessions but also during other recreational and leisure activities too!

Exercise Routinely

Ideally, a physically active person does either 30 minutes of moderately intense lifestyle activity every day of the week or 20 minutes of vigorous aerobic exercise three to five days a week. In fact, if you're fairly fit already, you should strive for both a lifestyle activity and a session of aerobic exercise nearly every day. As you become more fit, you will want to complement this routine with daily flexibility stretching exercises, plus strength-training exercises two to three times per week. When there's a choice, eliminate sedentary habits that require sitting for 30 minutes at a time.

STEPPING STONES

- Keep eating for nutrition, energy and general health.
- Eat slowly, choose small portions and stop when comfortably full.
- Maintain healthy eating habits by including a variety of foods and cutting back on fat, cholesterol, sugar and sodium.
- Keep drinking eight glasses of water per day.
- Make activity a lifetime mind-set.

- Continue your 30 minutes of moderate daily activity or 20 minutes of vigorous activity three to five days a week.
- Consider adding daily stretching and biweekly strength training.
- When possible, eliminate sedentary habits that require sitting for 30 minutes at a time.

Stepping Back

Pause, Study and Reflect

Read the following verses and consider the source of your physical strength:

> *For who is God except the Lord? Who but our God is a solid rock? God arms me with strength; he has made my way safe. He makes me as surefooted as a deer, leading me safely along the mountain heights. He prepares me for battle; he strengthens me to draw a bow of bronze.*
>
> (Psalm 18:31-34, *NLT*).

Stepping Forward

Make It Work for You

➳ Which of the Stepping Stones present the greatest challenge for you?

➳ List some ways to overcome these challenges.

TAKING AIM

SET REALISTIC GOALS

Focus, Results and Rewards

We've already noted that successful maintainers have written realistic goals and a plan for achieving them. While this ongoing, detailed planning may seem cumbersome at first, you'll find it a good investment. Your goals will help you stay focused, realistic and big-picture oriented. As you see results, those written goals will continue to be a source of encouragement as well as proof for both you and your First Place group members that you're staying the course. You'll also be able to plan for special rewards as you reach your goals.

Details, Direction and Determination

Your objectives should be detailed, including your healthy weight range, the corresponding daily calorie intake, your Live-It plan and a physical-activity plan. Plus, you must mentally commit to strive after these goals, acting on principle rather than whim, feelings or emotional needs. Just maintain the proper perspective you've so carefully cultivated: Food serves your physical needs so that your healthy physical body can serve the Lord. Keep first things first!

STEPPING STONES

- Written goals keep you focused, realistic and big-picture oriented.
- Written goals will continue to be a source of encouragement.
- Written goals help your First Place class hold you accountable.
- Goals should include a healthy weight range, your new calorie-intake level, the Live-It plan and a continuation of your activity plan.

STEPPING BACK

Pause, Study and Reflect

Consider the following passage:

So I run straight to the goal with purpose in every step. I am not like a boxer who misses his punches.
I discipline my body like an athlete, training it to do what it should. Otherwise, I fear that after
preaching to others I myself might be disqualified. (1 Corinthians 9:26,27, NLT)

➤ How would you characterize Paul's treatment of his physical body? Why did he do this?

➤ What does this principle mean for your goal setting?

STEPPING FORWARD

Make It Work for You

1. Set your new weight-range goal by completing the following table. This should be about a five-pound range, allowing for harmless fluid retention while also avoiding clothing size changes or metabolism imbalance.

Current New Weight	Five-Pound Fluctuation Window	My New Weight-Range Goal
_____ pounds	From _____ pounds above to _____ pounds below current new weight	From _____ pounds to _____ pounds

2. Next, refer to your adjusted BMR number in the Balancing Act section (p. 171). Use that number to complete the following:

    My new body requires _____ calories per day, at a _____ level of physical activity, to maintain my weight-range goal.

3. If your new calories-per-day level is *higher* than what you're currently consuming, simply add calories gradually. For example, if you've been eating 1,500 per day and your new adjusted BMR is 1,700, add 100 per week for two weeks in a row. Then simply stay at that level and observe your weight pattern to be certain it's stable.

4. Remember for weight maintenance, calories taken in must equal calories burned. Adding calories beyond your adjusted BMR or lowering your activity level will result in weight gain.

MY NEW DAILY EXCHANGE ALLOWANCES

On your CR, circle the daily exchange allowances corresponding to your new calorie level. Distribute your total allowable exchanges over each section below. Remember, if you're adding calories to your current level, do so at a rate of about 100 calories per week. This will require making copies and filling out graduated versions of this chart.

TAKING AIM: MY SAMPLE DAY

My New Live-It Plan at _____ Calories Per Day			
	Morning	Midday	Evening	Total
Bread/Starch				
Meat				
Vegetable				
Fruit				
Milk				
Fat				

Plan your sample week of activity according to the level you used in calculating your adjusted BMR. Daily stretching, three to five 30-minute aerobic exercise sessions and two strength training sessions are ideal.

MY ACTIVITY PLAN

	Mon	Tue	Wed	Thurs	Fri	Sat	Sun
Aerobic Exercise							
Stretches							
Strength Training							

KEEPING TRACK TO KEEP ON TRACK

Therefore let him who thinks he stands take heed lest he fall (1 Corinthians 10:12, NASB).

MONITOR YOUR STEPS

Admit the Flesh Is Weak

Paul's warning in 1 Corinthians refers to a time when, despite God's guidance through the desert, the Israelites were still prone to complain, considering the difficulties instead of the benefits and idolizing the visible rather than trusting the living God. We are no different today. The verse exhorts us to recognize our weaknesses and admit we're only as strong as our ability to lean on Him.

Take Stock

When we reach a goal, we often feel a false sense of security, strength and independence. This can lead to reliance on self-confidence instead of godly principles. So you need an honest evaluation of your condition and an objective assessment of your progress. The best way to do this honestly is to monitor your steps.

Specify Checkpoints

Remember, perfection is not the goal. The goal is a happy, effective, healthy life lived for God's glory. This includes a balance of prayer, Bible study, physical activity, eating habits, emotions and your weight. But that's a lot to keep track of, and your new maintenance goals may require conscious changes and ongoing adaptation. Thus it makes sense to not only write out your goals, but your checkpoints as well.

Checks and Balances

Regularly compare your status to your goals, adapting your plan as needed. Monitoring your new lifestyle will help you track your progress, stay honest with yourself and watch the Lord work! So keep an eye on your efforts by recording your daily progress in your CR, as suggested in the Stepping Forward application section that follows.

STEPPING STONES

- Your big-picture goal is a happy, effective, healthy life lived for God's glory.
- Related goals are numerous, so they're easiest to track when written.
- Honest evaluation of progress encourages dependence on Him.
- Your new maintenance goals will require conscious changes and continuous adaptation.
- Tracking your progress will help you stick with your plan throughout these changes.

STEPPING BACK

Pause, Study and Reflect

➤ List the Israelites' specific sins as enumerated in 1 Corinthians 10:1-14.

➤ List Paul's related warnings to the Corinthians.

➤ In which of these areas are you most tempted to sin when trying to achieve your goals?

Consider the real-life difficulties of sticking with your Live-It plan. Memorize 1 Corinthians 10:12,13 for those times when it's difficult to resist the temptation to stray from the program.

STEPPING FORWARD

Make It Work for You

Use your CR to record your daily progress in following your Live-It plan. Include your actual eating habits as well as your time in prayer, Bible study, Scripture reading, verse memorization and exercise.

ENCOURAGING ONE ANOTHER

STAY WITH YOUR FIRST PLACE GROUP

Support Means Success
By now you know the importance of people who support you. Don't minimize the importance of your existing First Place group just because you've reached your healthy-weight objective. As a Christian, you'll always benefit from godly counsel, encouragement and support—both from the Lord Jesus Himself and from your brothers and sisters in Christ. Besides, others will benefit from hearing of your growth and success because God designed us to live and grow within key relationships, beginning with our relationship with Him.

Look to the Lord
Take time now to review your relationships, beginning with your relationship with the Lord God Himself. He alone knows you, knows your future and has the power to change and develop you through His Holy Spirit. He's the primary source to look to. If there's some area of your life that you haven't entrusted to Him, now's the time to do so! And remember to request His wisdom for planning, as well as His strength for energetic, persevering service in your new lifestyle.

Talk to Your Team
Consider your ongoing partnerships with friends, family and your First Place group members. As you look toward the long haul, identify and list areas in which you might need help. Encourage your First Place group to provide advice, ideas, perspective, challenges, constructive criticism and incentives to change. Take the time to use your hard-earned lessons to inspire and support others who are just beginning their journey to fitness.

A Ready Reply
Of course, not everyone is as supportive as your group members, so remember that the key to handling difficult people is to look to the Lord—not others—for approval. Be prepared with helpful responses; become aware of those who tend to sabotage your weight control efforts by offering unhealthy food or extra helpings. Learn to say no thank you. And take a stand for what is right! Try turning the situation around: Rather than letting others influence you negatively, exhort them to do right!

Learning to Lead
By reaching your weight-loss goal in First Place, you are now equipped to share with others what God has taught you in the process. Pray about leading your own First Place group. Leadership will have a two-fold benefit. First, others will be inspired by your success. Second, as a leader you will have the accountability and encouragement of other leaders—and the group members you will lead—to maintain your own weight loss. You might begin by volunteering to assist your present First Place leader until you feel comfortable leading a group.

Do not conform any longer to the pattern of this world, but be transformed by the renewing of your mind. Then you will be able to test and approve what God's will is—his good, pleasing and perfect will (Romans 12:2).

STEPPING STONES

- As a Christian, you'll always need godly counsel, encouragement and support from the Body.
- Others will be strengthened and inspired by your success too.
- Now is a good time to review and strengthen key relationships, beginning with the Lord God Himself.
- Keys to handling difficult people include looking to the Lord (not others) for approval and being prepared with helpful responses.

STEPPING BACK

Pause, Study and Reflect

➽ According to James 1:5, in what areas can God's wisdom help you, as you move forward?

➽ Read Ephesians 4:15,16. What command is given to the members of the Body?

Speaking the truth in love, we are to grow up in all aspects into Him, who is the head, even Christ, from whom the whole body, being fitted and held together by that which every joint supplies, according to the proper working of each individual part, causes the growth of the body for the building up of itself in love (Ephesians 4:15,16 NASB).

➽ How does this come about, and why is this important?

STEPPING FORWARD

Make It Work for You

➤ Prayerfully consider the status of your own relationship with God. In which areas, if any, are you not trusting Him?

 Ask the Lord to help you maintain your First Place group relationships in such a way as to build up His Body and bring Him glory.

➤ Think of typically difficult people and tough situations in your desire to live a healthy lifestyle. Write some helpful responses, and ask God to help you respond accordingly.

BECOMING AN OVERCOMER

SHARPEN YOUR SWORD IN ADVANCE

Difficulty, but Not Disaster
In the real world, you can't control your circumstances, but you can control your responses to them. Besides, the Lord often uses difficult situations to conform us to His Son, prune us, refocus us on His priorities and teach us to depend on Him. So expect difficulties and plan to let them be learning experiences instead of disasters. Then when they do come, ask Him for help and follow His plan.

Plan for Problems
Snags and obstacles in your weight maintenance program may include temptations, illness or injury, major life changes, crises, holidays, vacations, special occasions, your job, stress or even plain old bad weather. So be proactive. Think through situations in which you'd be likely to jump ship and abandon your healthy eating and lifestyle. Then consider specific plans for dealing with these challenges. You don't have to give in to temptation because He will provide a way out right at the time you are tempted. Just ask!

Forgive and Forget
And if you do have a setback, a binge or a bad day, don't throw in the towel! Just ask Him to help you forgive yourself, learn from it, adjust your plan and get back into the race.

STEPPING STONES

- You can't control circumstances, but you can control your responses.
- The Lord uses difficult situations to conform us to His Son.
- Difficulties and obstacles are guaranteed.
- Have a proactive plan.
- If you have a setback, don't quit; learn from it and move on.

STEPPING BACK

Pause, Study and Reflect

➤ According to Hebrews 12:1-11, what is the main point of suffering, the main perspective God wants us to have during trials and the result of trials to which we respond rightly?

Underline the phrase in Ephesians 6:10-12 that tells you what kind of armor you need. Why do we need this armor?

Finally, be strong in the Lord, and in the strength of His might. Put on the full armor of God, that you may be able to stand firm against the schemes of the devil. For our struggle is not against flesh and blood, but against the rulers, against the powers, against the world forces of this darkness, against the spiritual forces of wickedness in the heavenly places (Ephesians 6:10-12, NASB).

STEPPING FORWARD

Make It Work for You

What trials have you overcome in developing your new healthy lifestyle?

What verses encouraged you?

How did the Lord God use the trials to refine you?

Consider the right response to these potential trials, and write out your practical strategy.

KEEPING FIRST THINGS FIRST

I . . . entreat you to walk in a manner worthy of the calling
with which you have been called (Ephesians 4:1, NASB).

WALK IN A WORTHY WAY

Service, Not Self

Now that you're armed with these reminders about weight control, goals and monitoring, you might be tempted to place too much emphasis on self each day. It's easy to focus on the program, your body image and your goal charts, but remember that these are merely tools to assist you in building lifelong healthy habits—they are not ends in themselves. It's far more important to focus on using your newfound energy and bearing spiritual fruit for the Lord.

Study for Success

That's why continued daily prayer and Bible study are so critical for your long-term success. Prayer in the Spirit communicates with Him in worship, in petition and with gratitude. Bible study is the primary means by which He reveals His truth to us—through careful, accurate study of His Word. So, if you haven't already done so, commit to a lifelong habit of daily quiet time, ensuring continual dependence on His wisdom. You'll soon find that you can discern what is pleasing to Him, align your steps with His will and know that you are keeping Him in first place.

Stay the Course

As you can see, your new maintenance program isn't new after all. You actually learned and incorporated these principles during your First Place studies. Now is simply a good time to review the facts, remember your motives, look to the Lord for endurance and learn to press on. The result? Lifelong healthy eating, physical activity and energetic service to God. One day at a time, you can stay the course!

Grace and peace be multiplied to you in the knowledge of God and of Jesus our Lord; seeing that His
divine power has granted to us everything pertaining to life and godliness, through the true knowledge
of Him who called us by His own glory and excellence (2 Peter 1:2,3, NASB).

STEPPING STONES

- While goals are important, do not let them cause self-absorption. Instead, focus on bearing spiritual fruit for the Lord.
- Continued daily prayer and Bible study are essential to your long-term success.
- Maintenance doesn't involve anything new: It's simply a time to review facts, remember motives, look to the Lord for endurance and learn tools for pressing on toward the long-term goal.

Stepping Back

Pause, Study and Reflect

- ➤ After reading Hebrews 4:12, list the specific attributes stated about God's Word. Consider how these can help you grow spiritually.

- ➤ List the attributes of God's Word found in 2 Timothy 3:16,17. Consider how these can help you grow spiritually.

Stepping Forward

Make It Work for You

- ➤ List obstacles you've run into regarding consistent daily prayer and Bible study time.

KEEPING FIRST THINGS FIRST: MY PRIORITY REVIEW

Use the following chart to identify your real priorities. Then make adjustments as needed, putting first things first. Fill out the chart, adding your own activities to the list. Then, check *T* for activities with temporal value and *E* for those of eternal value.

Daily Activities List	Time Spent	T	E	Adjustment Required?
Bible study				
Prayer				
Exercise				
Work				
Family time				
Chores				
Church				
Others				

Inspiration &Information Every Month!

Subscribe Today!

Every newsletter gives you:
- ## New recipes
- ## Helpful articles
- ## Food tips
- ## Inspiring testimonies
- ## Coming events
- ## And much more!

Register for our FREE e-newsletter at www.firstplace.org

A Must-Have Publication for all First Place Leaders & Members!

To receive information about special events & products

Stay in the Loop!
Register Your Group!

Visit us online at
www.firstplace.org
or return the form to the right

First Place Group Registration Form

First name _____ Last name _____
❏ Member   ❏ Leader
Address _____
City   State _____ Zip _____
Phone Number (____) _____
E-mail Address (____) _____
Church Name (where group is located) _____
Church Address _____
City   State _____ Zip _____
Church Phone Number (____) _____
Church Fax Number (____)_____
Church E-mail Address _____
Name of Group Leader_____

Three Easy Ways to Register Your Group:
Online: www.firstplace.org
Mail: 2300 Knoll Drive, Ventura Ca 93003-7383
Fax: (805) 289-0215

11060

First Place was founded under the providence of God and with the conviction that there is a need for a program which will train the minds, develop the moral character and enrich the spiritual lives of all those who may come within the sphere of its influence.

First Place is dedicated to providing quality information for development of a physical, emotional and spiritual environment leading to a life that honors God in Jesus Christ. As a health-oriented program, First Place will stress the highest excellence and proficiency in instruction with a goal of developing within each participant mastery of all the basics of a lasting healthy lifestyle, so that all may achieve their highest potential in body, mind and spirit. The spiritual development of each participant shall be given high priority so that each may come to the knowledge of Jesus Christ and God's plan and purpose for each life.

First Place offers instruction, encouragement and support to help members experience a more abundant life. Please contact the First Place national office in Houston, Texas at (800) 727-5223 for information on the following resources:

❖ Training Opportunities

❖ Conferences/Rallies

❖ Workshops

❖ Fitness Weeks

Send personal testimonies to:

First Place
7401 Katy Freeway
Houston, TX 77024

Phone: **(800) 727-5223**
Website: ***www.firstplace.org***

Bible Studies to Help You Put Christ First

Giving Christ First Place
Bible Study
ISBN 08307.28643

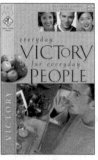

Everyday Victory for Everyday People
Bible Study
ISBN 08307.28651

Life Under Control
Bible Study
ISBN 08307.29305

Life That Wins
Bible Study
ISBN 08307.29240

Seeking God's Best
Bible Study
ISBN 08307.29259

Pressing On to the Prize
Bible Study
ISBN 08307.29267

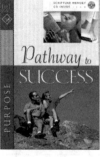

Pathway to Success
Bible Study
ISBN 08307.29275

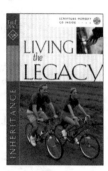

Living the Legacy
Bible Study
ISBN 08307.29283

Making Wise Choices
Bible Study
ISBN 08307.30818

Begin Again
Bible Study
ISBN 08307.32330

Living in Grace
Bible Study
ISBN 08307.32349

A New Creation
Bible Study
ISBN 08307.33566

Healthy Boundaries
Bible Study
ISBN 08307.38002

Choosing Thankfulness
Bible Study
ISBN 08307.38185

Available at bookstores everywhere or by calling
1-800-4-GOSPEL. **Join the First Place community
and order products at www.firstplace.org.**

Gospel Light

First Place products are available from your Gospel Light supplier

First Place Resource Order Form

TITLE	ISBN/SPCN	QTY	PRICE	ITEM TOTAL
First Place Group Starter Kit ($198 Value!)	08307.28708		149.99	
First Place Member's Kit ($101 Value!)	08307.28694		79.99	
First Place (Lewis/Whalin) (included in Group Starter Kit)	08307.28635		18.99	
Choosing to Change (Lewis) (included in Member's and Group Starter Kits)	08307.28627		8.99	
Giving Christ First Place Bible Study w/Scripture Memory Music CD (included in Group Starter Kit)	08307.28643		19.99	
Everyday Victory for Everyday People Bible Study w/Scripture Memory Music CD	08307.28651		19.99	
Life That Wins Bible Study w/ Scripture Memory Music CD	08307.29240		19.99	
Life Under Control Bible Study w/ Scripture Memory Music CD	08307.29305		19.99	
Pressing On to the Prize Bible Study w/ Scripture Memory Music CD	08307.29267		19.99	
Seeking God's Best Bible Study w/ Scripture Memory Music CD	08307.29259		19.99	
Living the Legacy Bible Study w/ Scripture Memory Music CD	08307.29283		19.99	
Pathway to Success Bible Study w/ Scripture Memory Music CD	08307.29275		19.99	
Prayer Journal (included in Member's Kit)	08307.29003		9.99	
Motivational Audiocassettes (pkg. of 4) (included in Member's Kit)	607135.005988		29.99	
Commitment Records (pkg. o f 13) (included in Member's Kit)	08307.29011		6.99	
Scripture Memory Verses: Walking in the Word (included in Member's Kit)	08307.28996		14.99	
Leader's Guide (included in Group Starter Kit)	08307.28678		19.99	
Food Exchange Plan Video (included in Group Starter Kit)	607135.006138		29.99	
Orientation Video (included in Group Starter Kit)	607135.005940		29.99	
Nine Commitments Video (included in Group Starter Kit)	607135.005957		39.99	
Giving Christ First Place Scripture Memory Music CD	607135.005902		9.99	
Giving Christ First Place Scripture Memory Music Cassette	607135.005919		6.99	
Everyday Victory for Everyday People Scripture Memory Music CD	607135.005926		9.99	
Everyday Victory for Everyday People Scripture Memory Music Cassette	607135.005933		6.99	
Life Under Control Scripture Memory Music CD	607135.006213		9.99	
Life Under Control Scripture Memory Music Cassette	607135.006206		6.99	
Life That Wins Scripture Memory Music CD	607135.006237		9.99	
Life That Wins Scripture Memory Music Cassette	607135.006220		6.99	
Seeking God's Best Scripture Memory Music CD	607135.006244		9.99	
Seeking God's Best Scripture Memory Music Cassette	607135.006251		6.99	
Pressing On to the Prize Scripture Memory Music CD	607135.006268		9.99	
Pressing On to the Prize Scripture Memory Music Cassette	607135.006275		6.99	
Pathway to Success Scripture Memory Music CD	607135.006282		9.99	
Pathway to Success Scripture Memory Music Cassette	607135.006299		6.99	
Living the Legacy Scripture Memory Music CD	607135.006305		9.99	
Living the Legacy Scripture Memory Music Cassette	607135.006312		6.99	

PRICES SUBJECT TO CHANGE.   11052   **Total : $_____**

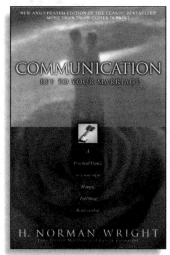
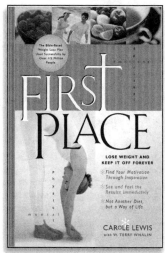

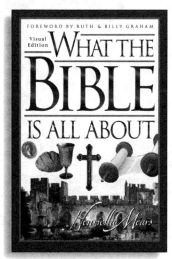
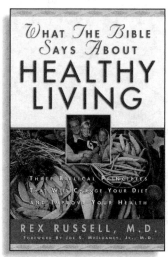
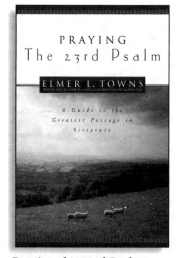

Also from Carole Lewis

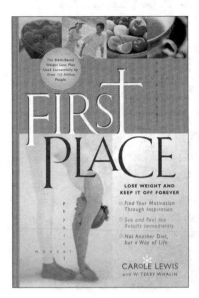
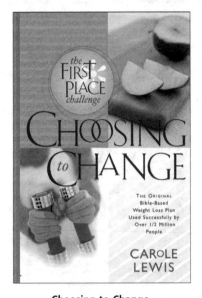
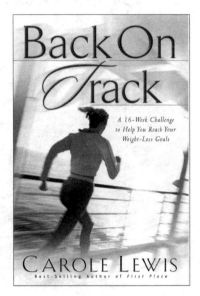

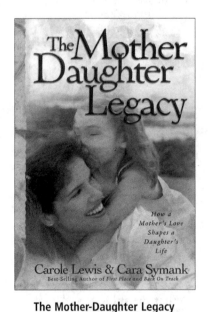
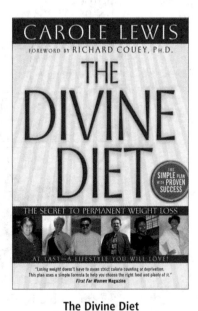